In Defence of LIBERALISM

In Defence of LIBERALISM

K. M. Panikkar

GYAN

Published by

Gyan Publishing House
5, Ansari Road
Daryaganj, New Delhi-110002
Phone: 011-47034999, 9811692060
E-mail: books@gyanbooks.com

Distribution Network
gyanbooks.com
India, USA, Canada, UK, Australia

ISBN: 978-81-212-5543-1 (HB)
First Published, 1962

2nd Impression 2024

Printed at: Gyan Press, Delhi.

IN DEFENCE OF LIBERALISM
Author: K. M. PANIKKAR

In Defence of LIBERALISM

In Defence of LIBERALISM

K. M. PANIKKAR

Issued under the auspices of the Indian School of International Studies

ASIA PUBLISHING HOUSE
BOMBAY • CALCUTTA • NEW DELHI • MADRAS
LONDON • NEW YORK

PREFACE

IT gives me great pleasure to introduce the Sarojini Naidu Lectures to the public. These lectures have been instituted in memory of Mrs. Sarojini Naidu who presided with great distinction over the Asian Relations Conference 1947. The Indian School of International Studies thought it appropriate to arrange a series of lectures every year on some significant subject relating to international relations —political, economic, cultural—which would, of course, be of significance to Asia as well. The key-note of Mrs. Sarojini Naidu's life and work was harmony; that is what is needed most in the world of today and I have no doubt that a series of lectures by persons distinguished in public life and scholarship will stimulate constructive thinking on international problems in the understanding of which the School is specially interested. Among those who have accepted the invitation of the School to deliver the lectures are, Sardar K. M. Panikkar, Vice-Chancellor, Jammu and Kashmir University, Mrs. Vijay Laxmi Pandit, former President of the United Nations General Assembly and Mr. M. C. Setalvad, Attorney General of India.

The School is grateful to Asia Publishing House

for their generous endowment which has made it possible for us to institute the lectures

A. APPADORAI
Director

Indian School of International Studies
New Delhi
12 April 1962

CONTENTS

INTRODUCTION

THE School of International Studies did me the honour of inviting me to deliver the Sarojini Naidu Memorial Lectures for 1961 Poet, national leader, fighter in the cause of India's freedom, champion of women's rights, President of the National Congress and finally Governor of India's largest state, Mrs Sarojini Naidu occupied a place of unique honour in the life of modern India People called her Mother India, and in a way the sobriquet was just as she might be said to have embodied in her person the spirit and genius of India

Throughout her political life she was associated with the Indian National Congress but in her political faith she was a liberal, not in the sense of belonging to the party which appropriated that name, but of upholding the great doctrines associated with the creed of liberalism—the worth of individual and the protection of his personality, freedom of speech, thought and association, tolerance, the dissociation of religion from politics, a secular approach to social and political issues, and an abiding faith in man's capacity to progress A humanist in the fullest sense of the word, she approached the political problems of her time with an open mind and contributed much to the spirit of tolerance and understanding which India has been endeavouring to put into practice in her political life The choice of my subject—In Defence of Liberalism—for her memorial lectures I am sure, would have met with her approval

In the lectures that follow I have dealt with the liberal doctrines their growth eclipse and fulfilment by general acceptance over large areas in Europe, America and Asia, but I have only alluded briefly and *enpassant* to the position of liberal thought in India Nor have I, in view of the unavoidable limitation of time allowed for the lectures, dealt with the integral relationship of liberal thought with the idea of progress except in a casual way

So far as Indian liberalism is concerned, as I have pointed out in the fourth lecture, it is made up of two distinct streams each of which has a fairly long history Ram Mohan Roy, the father of liberalism in India, was a contemporary of Bentham He was in contact with advanced European thought at the time and in a measure it inspired him in his activities He laid the foundation of the movement for the social transformation of the Hindus, basing himself on the principles of equality and individual judgement Apart from the religious reform which he initiated, which was also a reflection of the liberal spirit, Ram Mohan may well claim that by emphasising the right of women to freedom, the necessity of western education and of the establishment of a casteless society he had started the Hindu people on the road of liberal transformation Though it was a limited movement confined originally to Bengal and there also to the middle classes, its contribution to the growth of liberal thought in India became significant with the spread of English language as the medium of cultural communication throughout India

Keshab Chandra Sen, Mahadev Govind Ranade and others all over India contributed in the middle of the century to the growth of the liberal spirit But more significant than all of them was Swami Vivekananda, *a heroic figure who introduced into* orthodox Hinduism the spirit of social justice His unique contribution to the growth of the liberal spirit in India was his emphasis on the dissociation of social institutions from religion He proclaimed all over India the truth that such institutions as caste and prohibitions like widow remarriage were merely social practices and were fundamentally unconnected with Hindu religion He emphasised that their reformation was essentially a matter of social justice This was indeed a basic contribution to Indian liberal thought, for without this separation the reform of Hindu society according to the liberal principles would not have been possible The great social reform movement culminating in the far reaching legislation covering all aspects of

Hindu life, which constituted one of the achievements of Republican India, was rendered possible by the teachings of Swami Vivekananda

The Congress as a national movement was interested primarily in the achievement of freedom and included in its ranks all shades of political opinion which whatever their social ideals, accepted freedom to be India's political goal The nature of that freedom was not at first a matter with which the Congress as a body concerned itself But with the ascendancy of Gandhiji the situation underwent a change He introduced a programme of political action which in some of its aspects was based on the ideas for which liberalism stood The abolition of untouchability, the equality of women, the rationalisation of labour-capital relations, universal franchise, these were the essentially liberal aspects of his programme They maintained and strengthened the liberal character of the national movement But it has to be recognised that the methods which he evolved and used with such effect, though revolutionary in character and had wide democratic results in that they woke up the masses from their time old slumber, were in many respects irreconcileable with liberal thought More especially, picketing, mass Satyagraha, hunger strike and other similar weapons in the Gandhian armoury, though justifiable as peaceful methods of revolt against an oppressive alien regime which deprived people of their freedom, could hardly be claimed as upholding liberal ideas or strengthening the democratic character of the national movement Our experience of these methods after independence, when for getting every minor local complaint settled public men have advocated Satyagraha or gone on "fasts unto death', should amply prove that however much we might admire the Gandhian technique, we could not consider it as a welcome addition to our political tradition

This was however only one aspect of the nationlist movement under Mahatma Gandhi Apart from such items of the national platform as the abolition of untouchability, already alluded to, the Congress movement by fighting vigorously the encroachment of the Government on public liberties—limitations on personal freedom, restrictions on the press, attempts to interfere with the judiciary—held aloft the banner of liberalism It should be remembered that one of the major factors which changed public opinion in India in favour of Mahatma Gandhi s programme was the attempt of the British Indian Government, immediately after the first Great War, to perpetuate through legislation (the Rowlatt Act) the arbitrary powers they had assumed during war time The Rowlatt Act was the most massive assault on public freedom that the British Government attempted in India The public resistance under Mahatma Gandhi to this most illiberal legislation was one of the factors that changed the character of Indian Nationalism

The political liberalism of the national movement was overshadowed no less by its revolutionary character than by some of the other aspects of Gandhian economy like *khaddar*, emphasis on village work austerity in living, etc These, however, did not affect the basic liberalism of the movement which continued at all times to emphasise the rights of the individual and the value of essential freedoms, the rule of law, secularism in politics and faith in social justice On this last, the insistence of the Congress on the total abolition of untouchability is a shining instance As we shall show in the course of the lectures, secularism in the sense of the separation of religion from the state was always a major feature of liberal thought From the time of the American Declaration of Independence, which lays down that there shall be no official religion in the United States, this has been considered a part of the liberal ideal, though in England, in view of the special relations of the crown with the established church, a considerable time had to elapse before the Non conformists, Catholics Jews and others could attain equality in civil matters with members of the Anglican Church In India, however, the nationalist movement, from the very beginning, became the champion of the secular state, in which each one of the many religions practised in India would have equal rights and none would enjoy state patronage or support It should be remembered that till 1947 India had an established official religion and that was Christianity whose establishment was paid for by the Government of India. Gentlemen assuming territorial dignities like Thomas "Calcutta," Henry "Madras' and John "Bombay" claimed spiritual jurisdiction under the authority of the King of England over the territories of India and were maintained in their "palaces" from state revenues In a country where the Anglican population was but a microscopic minority this was ridiculously pretentious From the beginning it was obvious that once India was free she could not have an official religion not only because of her liberal approach but because of large and important religious minorities which existed all over India—Muslims, Sikhs, Christians, Buddhists and Parsis

There was another stream which added strength and volume to Indian liberal thought and that came strangely enough from the British administration When after the period of conquest, the East India Company began, in the twenties of the 19th century, to settle down to regular administrative work, Benthamite liberalism had begun to have a great deal of influence in intellectual circles in England This began in a measure to be reflected in the administration of India—at least in those spheres which did not immediately affect the security of British rule Lord William Bentinck was the first statesman associated with the Benthamite school in India, but its most eminent representative in every way was the historian and liberal politician, Thomas Babington Macaulay Macaulay was responsible for two major aspects of British liberal policy in India, an education based not only on English but on modern knowledge, mainly emphasising humanities, and secondly the great Indian Penal Code which for the first time established the doctrine of equality of all before law Besides, the establishment of High Courts under royal charter, introducing not only the principles of the common law but also the right of enforcement of liberties through writs, secured for India the inestimable privilege of the supremacy of law over the executive, which is one of the basic principles of the liberal state However much in matters affecting security, sedition (or in some cases even racial prejudice) they may have occasionally fallen from their high ideals, the High Courts in India, generally speaking, upheld the individual's rights and the equality before law of all people without reference to caste, creed or status Also they became in time the visible symbols of the supremacy of law which is the basic characteristic of the liberal state

It is not only the British legal system that was a major factor in the broad acceptance of liberal thought in India The system of education, the foundation of which was again laid by Macaulay, though its imposing structure was erected later by Sir Charles Wood, and by the three great Universities—Calcutta, Bombay and Madras—established in 1857, was so designed as to import into India lock, stock and barrel, the prevailing opinions in England, which at the time and for half a century to come were predominantly liberal University education in India was not only through English, but the main subjects taught for many decades were English literature, British and European history, political economy and other humanistic courses It is only after the first Great War that science subjects became major courses of study in Indian Universities One of the dominant trends in English literature in the 19th century was a glorification of liberty and the Whig interpretation of British history, then considered authoritative, was orientiated towards liberalism, both of which therefore came to India with the force of a new revelation

During the latter half of the 19th and the first two decades of the 20th century the only major profession open to Indians was law Medical and engineering colleges were few The majority of graduates from the Universities thronged to the law colleges The doctrines of law they studied there were also based on British jurisprudence and legal thought More especially British constitutional law as interpreted for them was a record of liberal achievement As the political leaders till the time of Mahatma Gandhi (including him and his chief associates) came mainly from among successful lawyers and jurists, their approach to political issues was coloured by the constitutional doctrines and practices of England Thus the British precedents and political doctrines which in the 19th century had taken a definitely liberal colouring became an integral part of the political and constitutional thought of India

Another development which was instrumental in gaining for liberalism a widespread acceptance in India's intellectual life was the large scale migration of students from all parts of India to England for higher education It should be remembered that till after the first Great War the only door of entry into the superior civil services in India was through competitive examinations held in England The dominant ambition of the middle classes till almost the end of the British rule in India was to secure admission to the civil services and consequently from about 1880 the brighter students from Indian

Universities began to seek admission in London Oxford, Cambridge and other seats of learning Other courses, especially law, medicine and engineering, also attracted a considerable number As the last quarter of the 19th and the first fifteen years of the 20th century marked the apogee of liberalism, intellectual opinion in India became stamped with the thought of Mill, Spencer, Graham Wallas and Hobson and the constitutional theories of Bagehot Dicey and Anson

The weakness of Indian liberalism which was woven out of these strands was that it was confined to a small class—to a little group of intelligentsia which came from the middle classes It was, so to say, a "Brahmin liberalism," which while proclaiming the equality of man, accepted caste, untouchability and other illiberal aspects of Hinduism Sri Ramesh Chandra Mitra, a spokesman of this class, in his welcome address to the Congress of 1896 stated the principle thus "The educated community represented the brain and conscience of the country and was the legitimate spokesman of the illiterate masses, the natural custodian of their interests It is true in all ages those who think must govern those who toil"

This doctrine of a limited liberalism received its *coup de grace* only with Gandhiji But even before the Mahatma's appearance on the Indian scene liberalism had shown signs of bursting the limitations of caste In Madras Dr T M Nair had in 1915 started a movement against the dominance of caste and especially of the Brahmins The non-Brahmin movement was reactionary in its politics but its social ideals were those of a liberal democracy in which the non Brahmin classes, so long under the social religious and political domination of the Brahmins would shake off the bondage of caste Though the movement was based on a hatred of the Brahmins, which was systematically worked up by political propaganda, the non-Brahmin movement may be said to have been the first awakening of the lower classes in the South The official name of the party which represented the movement was the South Indian Liberal Federation The newspaper which voiced its views was known as *Justice,* indicating the principle of social justice for which it stood

The non-Brahmin movement was more or less confined to Madras Also, it was intolerant in its political activities, especially in its attitude towards the Brahmins Though it had considerable significance in the South, it could not by itself broaden the basis of Indian liberalism An all India movement, which was national and tolerant and at the same time revolutionary, was necessary if Indian liberalism was not to remain the doctrine of an intellectual group The attack on caste untouchability, the disabilities of women and other basically illiberal aspects of Hindu life had to be on a wider and more national front and this was what the non cooperation movement of Mahatma Gandhi did The twenty five years of the Gandhian movement not only brought women to the front rank of the national struggle undermined caste and untouchability, but it also broke down the resistance of feudalism entrenched in the princely states By the time independence was achieved Indian liberal thought had broadened its basis and had become a strong and unchallenged tradition in Indian political life

There was one aspect of British liberal thought which from the beginning Indians refused to accept and that was free trade It was clear to Indian political leaders that free trade which British liberalism elevated to the position of an economic dogma was no more than a translation into general terms of Britain s industrial and economic interests From the beginning Indian liberal thinking adopted a theory of moderate protection for local industries which the country was able to enforce only after the reforms of 1919, when the Central Indian Legislature came to have an Indian majority That economic protectionism was in no sense anti liberal or reactionary was clear from the fact that

America had always considered it an essential part of her economic policy Private enterprise, protected by tariffs, was the orthodox economic doctrine of Indian liberalism, reflecting the interests of the newly developing industrial classes

This approach to economic policy based on the liberal idea of *laissez faire* and protection underwent a change in the early thirties when for the first time Marxian thinking began seriously to penetrate Indian politics Both from the side of the communists and of the socialists, the liberal economic ideas of free enterprise came under attack Also, trade unionism began to take root in the country So far as the socialist attack was concerned, it was mostly directed against the outmoded economic views of Victorian liberalism of which India seemed to be the last refuge While firmly upholding and indeed championing the major liberal freedoms, the left wing nationalist opinion of India rejected the *laissez faire* doctrines and became the advocates of a planned society Instead of believing in the state which administered the least, as Mahatma Gandhi did, the new nationalists under the influence of socialist thinking, even when they were not socialists, welcomed the doctrine of the welfare state with its immense extension of administrative functions

Thus when India achieved her independence, the

liberal basis of the national movement consisted of four principal ideas Social justice involving large scale reorganisation of society meant to eliminate the inequalities and oppressions under which Indian social system had groaned for so long a time; the maintenance of civil freedoms—freedom of speech, liberty of person, etc which all liberals accepted as the basic assumptions of their view of society, a planned economy the object of which was ultimately to eliminate economic inequalities both by a rapid industrialisation of the country and by the utilisation of the powers of government for ensuring a better distribution of wealth, and fourthly the acceptance of the ideal of a welfare state which provides every individual with opportunities for his fullest development This comprehensive and organic conception of liberalism which was to find expression in the Indian Constitution and which, with all the imperfections inherent in the realisation of political programmes, remains the policy of the Indian Government goes, it will be conceded much beyond what the great liberals of the past had considered to be their doctrines For example, it includes both kinds of freedom, the old freedoms *of*, i e freedom of speech, of association, etc as well as the new freedoms *from*, i e freedom from hunger etc It not only accepts but also welcomes greatly increased activity of the state in fact the new liberalism of which India is an example discards the old fear of state action and bases its economic and social policies on state's own initiative and action

So far as India is concerned this is not an unplanned development These doctrines are enshrined in the Constitution in the Preamble, in the chapter on Fundamental Rights, and in the section dealing with directives of state policy The emphasis on "Justice social, economic and political," on "Liberty of thought, expression belief faith and worship, equality of status and opportunity and fraternity assuring the dignity of the individual" which is the characteristic of this unique declaration is clearly an affirmation of liberal faith It adds justice to the French revolutionary principles of equality, liberty and fraternity, defines liberty comprehensively, includes in its conception of equality not only equality of opportunity but of status In fact it is a more comprehensive enunciation of liberal principles than is available in any previous document

The primacy given to justice (which finds no place either in the Declaration of Independence or in the French Revolutionary slogans) is specially significant It is not merely the justice of the courts, but justice, social, economic and political that the Constitution seeks to secure for its citizens

It may be objected that declarations in the

Preamble are no more than expressions of pious hope, vague aspirations towards liberalism, and do not constitute any rights But the Constitution itself gives sanction and embodies as law many of the ideas proclaimed in the Preamble There is incorporated in the Constitution a declaration of Fundamental Rights The first part of this declaration which includes the rights relating to equality, liberty, freedom of conscience, provisions against employment of children under 14 in factories and mines and guarantees the rights relating to religion, is an effective and most important chapter in the law of the land enforceable through courts of law It includes all the essential rights of a citizen in a liberal state

Without proper and adequate sanctions, provision of human rights, however specific, will have but little meaning In this matter the Indian Constitution leans heavily on British and American practice the British system of writs by judicial courts, of *habeas corpus mandamus*, *certiorari*, *quo warranto* etc and the American practice of moving the Federal Court for the maintenance of rights provided in the Constitution This double insurance effectively safeguards the liberties of the individual in India and gives substance to the liberal doctrines en shrined in the declaration of fundamental rights

Granted that the Indian Constitution embodies

the essential principles of liberalism and provides India with the framework of a liberal state, the question still remains whether in the last twelve years that India has worked this Constitution she has upheld the liberal principles which she embodied in her formal declarations It is undoubtedly true that India has opted for planned economic development, involving large-scale interference in the economic activities of people and that she has fast transformed herself into an administering state, operating through an army of functionaries claiming to control almost everything from family planning to temple funds Even the village organisations, which had remained unaffected through all previous changes of government, have now been taken under the effective control of the leviathan state, which through the new programme of *panchyat raj* seeks to penetrate to the farthest corners of the land It is being freely alleged by its opponents that whatever its professions, the Indian Government is fast being transformed into an illiberal, centralised, totalitarian government under parliamentary forms

To a liberal of the first half of the 19th century, of the time of Cobden and Bright, this criticism would undoubtedly seem to be just But as I have sought to show in the concluding sections of these lectures, liberalism as a dynamic doctrine of politics has itself been undergoing radical change in form and content The liberalism of the Lloyd George period in England and of Roosevelt's New Deal flowed no doubt from the earlier doctrines but differed radically from the liberalism of the earlier generations The question today is not whether the state's activity has become all embracing, but whether the freedoms on which the liberal state is founded have a content far wider and deeper than in the past There can be no doubt that so far as India is concerned not only have the freedoms not been interfered with but they have been expanded to include every section of the community This is the significance of the *panchayat raj* or the great devolution of power now being undertaken India in fact is exploring new fields of liberal action

That civilisation can, through human effort, be made to move in a certain direction is the faith of liberalism That it should be made to move in such a way as to ensure social justice, liberty, equality and other freedoms is the essential feature of liberal policy These two basic ideas of liberalism may be contested, as indeed they are, by important schools of thought, the first, as being no more than a faith without adequate evidence from the historical experience of man and the second the realisation of equality, being capable of achievement only through a complete and revolutionary reconstitution of economic life under proletarian dictatorship Such partisan views notwithstanding, the new liberalism, adjusting itself to the social forces of the day and reconciling itself to the changed conception of the state, will continue to be the source of inspiration and the guiding light for the great majority of mankind outside the communist countries And even when *it is overtaken and superseded,* as all ideas must necessarily be, its basic principles would have become transformed and assimilated into the general traditions of civilisation

I

THE LIBERAL DOCTRINES

LIBERALISM as a political philosophy and as a programme of social action was the most important political and social characteristic of the 19th century It dominated the thought of the best minds and provided inspiration for the legislative and political activity of the period which ended only with the first Great War It was the accepted and official doctrine of England, France and the United States and reflected the aspirations of progressive minds everywhere in empires like Austria, Russia and Turkey where autocratic monarchs ruled, no less than in subject countries like India where imperialism flourished Everywhere its doctrines were proclaimed with a sense of mission

From 1830 to 1914 the dominant factor in politics was thus the corpus of ideas generally known as liberalism The inspiration of much of the social progress of the period can also be traced to liberal thought Even the forces of reaction had during this period adapted to a large extent the ideas and accepted to a degree the coloration of liberalism There was however growing up, side by side with it; a new philosophy which in due course was destined to supplement it If the 19th century could be said to be predominantly the era of liberalism, it could with no less justice be described as the period during which seeds sown by Karl Marx began to sprout, first as social democracy and later as communism Though the significance of the fact that the Communist Manifesto was published in 1848 and the doctrine of socialism began to penetrate the intellectuals in the latter half of the century cannot be overlooked, the fact remains that it was liberal thought that provided the dynamism for social and political action till the first Great War left the world in ruins and also provided the world with the challenging philosophy of communism

I propose in the following lectures to discuss briefly the assumptions of liberalism, analyse the ideas and doctrines which were found potent enough to inspire generations of intellectuals indicate briefly its permanent achievements and discuss the reasons for its eclipse

Though some of the individual ideas which in their totality constitute the broad movement which we call liberalism could be traced back in history and identified in different countries and civilisations it is only in the 18th century that they came to be formulated as a political doctrine The importance of the individual in society, a cardinal feature of liberalism, exists in Confucian thought The betterment of man through social organisation was preached by Asoka. Toleration of opinion was a recognised feature of Indian life. Though these and other ideas may be said to have existed separately, their formulation as a consistent theory took place only in the 18th century. It may be said to have started as a vision of history and a philosophy of political relationship. From Ibn Khaldoun to Boussuet, history was viewed as the unfolding of God's plan on earth. The revival of that view in our day among others by Dawson and Collingwood is an interesting fact about which we shall comment later. This doctrine of God's purpose in history found authority and support in the Church and in organised religion which claiming the right of interpreting God's purposes became also the official censors of history and its judgements. The first to question this doctrine was Voltaire whose philosophic view of history may be said to have laid the foundations of liberal thought by emphasising the rational character of human development and by holding that mankind, but for the obstruction of the Church, the monarchy, the nobility, etc. would be moving steadily on the road to progress. This doctrine found its authoritative elaboration in Condorcet's *Outline of the Progress of Human Mind*, a book which, in the opinion of a recent writer, more than any other, exemplifies the classic liberal interpretation of history. Condorcet wrote his book while he was hiding from Jacobin terror It is an affirmation of faith in human progress What Condorcet has said in this connection constitutes a kind of dogma of liberalism and deserves to be quoted

> Doubtless man will never become immortal, but the progress of preventive medicine, more healthful food and lodging, a way of life that will develop the body through proper exercise without damaging it through over work and finally the destruction of the two most active causes of physical degeneracy, extreme poverty and extreme wealth, may bring a time when death shall be the result of the ever more gradual decay of vital forces '

The political doctrine behind this new philosophy of liberalism was provided by Jean Jacques Rousseau in the *Social Contract* It had also another source of inspiration in Locke, whose influence on Voltaire s political thinking deserves to be mentioned It is however the *Social Contract* that provided the dynamism for the new movement It is important to remember the significance of this book The medieval state was one which claimed the right of control and authority either for the Emperor or for the Pope but not for the people Its popular theory of authority was of a monarchy by divine right In a society dominated by feudal doctrines and subjected to the ever-increasing claims of the Church, such a theory, in so far as it helped to create a modern state, may even be considered as being progressive. The thinkers of the earlier period like Bodin and Hobbes who enquired into the nature of the state rejected all ideas of covenant and argued that "it is the distinguishing mark of the sovereign that he cannot in any way be subjected to the command of another, for it is he who makes law for the subject, abrogates law already made and amends obsolete law." (Bodin concerning Sovereignty). To writers before Rousseau the central point in regard to the state was the sovereign. So it can well be imagined what a bombshell the very first sentence with which Rousseau opens his book the *Social Contract*—that "Man is born free but everywhere he is in chains"—was to his contemporaries. What Rousseau proceeded to establish was that all power is derived from the people whose will is at all times sovereign. Man and his rights became with Rousseau the central factor of the state. The denial of the divine right of both kings and churches in the affairs of men became a basic doctrine with liberals after Rousseau.

If a view of history was provided by Voltaire, a doctrine of progress by Condorcet and a theory of political power by Rousseau, thus laying the foundations of liberal thought, the first actual political manifestation of liberalism came from America The Declaration of Independence contained the stirring words

> We hold these truths to be self evident That all men are created equal that they are endowed by their creator with certain inalienable rights that among these are life liberty and pursuit of happiness That to secure these rights governments are instituted among men deriving their just powers from the consent of the governed that whenever any form of government becomes destructive of these ends it is the right of the people to alter to abolish it and to institute new government, laying its foundation on such principles and organising its powers in such form as to them shall seem likely to affect their safety and happiness

This indeed is a classic statement of one aspect of liberalism It was further supplemented by the Bill of Rights (1791) which provided among other things for the secular character of the state for the liberty of person right to due processes of law, for speedy and public trial—in fact for the supremacy of law Amendment I which is the first clause of what is known as the Bill of Rights lays down

> Congress shall make no law respecting an

> establishment of religion, or prohibiting the free exercise thereof, of abridging the freedom of speech or of the press, or the rights of the people peaceably to assemble, and to petition the government for a redress of grievances"

Amendment IV secured the liberty of persons and provided

> 'the right of the people to be secure in their persons, houses, papers and effects against unreasonable searches and seizures shall not be violated '

No less important from the liberal point of view is the provision in Amendment VI "In all criminal prosecutions the accused shall enjoy the right to a speedy and public trial by an impartial jury of the state and district, etc"

It was in America that the liberal state came first into existence, though its doctrines were first stated by European thinkers There is an influential school of American writers, of which the most eminent representative is Prescott Webb, which holds that the liberal doctrines were the outcome of the experiences of what they call the Great Frontier, the spirit of adventurous pioneering which faced the wide open spaces of the new continent and built up a great civilisation there The spirit of individualism freedom from the status-dominated social structure of the West the sense of protest which took the major groups to the New World these among other things were the factors which contributed to the doctrines enshrined in the Declaration of Independence which became in time the doctrine of liberalism and democracy While the contribution of the United States to the growth of liberal principles must always rank high it is well to remember and emphasise that it is only one stream in the mighty current which in a great sweep transformed the political and social structure of the 19th century world

The next step in the emergence of liberalism was more dramatic and indeed more universal in its influence And that was the French Revolution which brought down to dust the most powerful European monarchy and proclaimed as its gospel the three principles of liberty equality and fraternity The limited content of these three slogans—in terms of the thought of the time—will be discussed later, but what was revolutionary in them was that for the first time they provided a basis for political and social organisation different from the status dominated church controlled organisations of the past While the influence of the truths proclaimed in the American Declaration of Independence spread gradually and indeed was heard for a long time only as a distant rumble, the revolutionary slogans of liberty, equality and fraternity echoed like thunder all over Europe

Only one component was missing in what was being shaped as the message of liberalism and that was its economic idea This was provided by Adam Smith in 1776 by the publication of the *Wealth of Nations*, that bible of *laissez-faire* which was to dominate economic thought for decades to come The contribution of the French physiocrats, especially of Quesnay and Mirabeau Pere could not also be overlooked

1776 was indeed a significant year in the birth of liberalism It could well be called the period of liberal gestation for it was the year which witnessed the American Declaration of Independence, the publication of the *Wealth of Nations*, Bentham's *Fragment on Civil Government* and the first volume of Gibbon's *History of the Decline and Fall of the Roman Empire*—each in varying degrees significant for the growth of liberal thought

Though the liberal doctrines found their general formulation before the French Revolution of 1789, the opening of the liberal era was postponed for a considerable time as a result of the excesses of the Jacobin terror and the Napoleonic wars that followed It is one of the significant facts of history that the period immediately following a violent revolution is always reactionary The quarter of a century of Revolutionary and Napoleonic upheavals was followed by a period of social, religious and political reaction It was the period of Chateaubriand s Genius of Christianity and De Maistre s book on the Pope of the Holy Alliance, of the suppression of popular movements everywhere Prince Metternich presided over the group of statesmen who saw in the principles of liberalism danger of every kind to the society they represented Castlereagh represented this point of view in English politics But the ideas which had erupted as a Revolution in France had become the common inheritance of the intelligentsia of Europe and could not long be held back Rendered respectable by legists and thinkers like Bentham and humanitarians like Shaftesbury and with reaction showing no signs of stabilising itself anywhere the principles of the Revolution formulated now as demands for reform began soon to assert themselves

If a period has to be marked out for the birth of liberalism as a European movement, I should unhesitatingly indicate it as comprising of the three years 1830–33 The flight of Charles X in France may be considered as the final victory of the Revolution, for the July monarchy which replaced it was, perhaps in a shadowy way, the embodiment of liberal principles Louis Philippe was, as the official phraseology went, not only king by the grace of God but also by the grace of the French people—a revolutionary change in monarchical theory In England it was the period not only of the great Reform Act which was the first hesitating step towards democracy, but also of the abolition of slavery, catholic emancipation (1829), the practical equality for dissenters and non-conformists with the followers of the established church From that time till the end of the great period of peace in 1914, liberalism was the political philosophy in power to such an extent that Emile Olivier, the last Prime Minister of Napoleon III, coined even the phrase—the "liberal empire"—to camouflage the declining autocracy of his master It was attacked on the rear by those believing in hereditary privileges, themselves gradually converted to a diluted liberalism, and its flanks were threatened by the fast developing doctrines of socialism, which again in Western Europe adopted many of the liberal postulates The only power which refused to compromise with liberalism was the catholic Church which not only denounced the doctrines of liberalism, but declared, in the famous *Syllabus* of 1864, that it was a grievous error to hold that the Pope should compromise with liberal principles [1] For

[1] The change that has come over the attitude of

nearly a century a single political doctrine held the field and helped to transform both society and politics

Before discussing the problem further it is important to analyse the ideas and postulates of liberalism and to know how they differed from what went before and from what followed The first and basic doctrine of liberal thought is the value of the individual and consequently liberalism holds that the primary duty of the state is to ensure a man s freedom not only against encroachments of the sovereign but also of other organisations claiming the individual s allegiance Liberalism was originally conceived as the politics of individualism though we shall show that with the change in the character of the state and society at a later period, this individualistic approach was greatly modified The idea of placing the individual in the centre of politics was something new and strange in a society dominated by status Even in the 18th century in continental societies and to some extent even in England the worth of an

the Holy See itself in regard to liberalism may be seen from the recent encyclical *Mater et Magistra* (1961) which supplements the earlier pronouncement *quadrigesimo anno* (1931) *Mater et Magistra* goes to the extent of supporting nationalisation of industry in the interests of efficiency and cooperatives on democracy—indeed a far cry from the spirit of the *Syllabus* and even of *Rerum Novarum*

individual was related to the class he belonged Even in the Church, though a man born outside the nobility may in rare instances rise high, the great dignitaries were almost invariably drawn from the higher classes

The liberal idea was that the state should interfere as little as possible with the individual and his activities Suspicion of state power continued till the very end to be an essential element of liberalism, even after the liberal state had become gradually transformed in its declining days into a vast administering machine The second characteristic which is in some ways related to the importance attached to the individual, was the emphasis on civil liberties Freedom of person, speech, conscience, assembly, organisation, etc which modern democracies take for granted were not the characteristics of states anywhere before the days of liberalism In France the King could send any one to the Bastille or any other state prison without trial The bed of justice, *le lit de justice*, was a simple enough procedure for the king to override the privileges of the highest It should be remembered that it was a time when a man like Voltaire could be subjected with impunity to physical violence by an irate cadet of a noble house The common peasantry enjoyed no rights at all against the nobility or the king's officers, and thus in France, even then the most advanced of continental nations In England the position was no doubt a little better, but the legal system was oppressive enough against the common man in relation to the landowner

So far as freedom of speech was concerned the controversy in respect of Wilks and the North Briton would show that even in England the principle was by no means accepted as a general political right

Except in the United States which was originally the sanctuary of those persecuted for their religious views, no country in Europe recognised any such principle as freedom of conscience The revocation of the Edict of Nantes by Louis XIV had reaffirmed the exclusively catholic character of the French state In England, the Dissenters were discriminated against in many ways So far as the Catholics were concerned their disabilities were of a crying character As late as 1753 the British Parliament passed a law called Lord Hardwick's Act under which no one could be legally married in England except in the Church of England How revolutionary it was to proclaim as a doctrine, as the Bill of Rights did, that there shall be no official religion in the U S A can now be realised in the light of these facts

The liberal doctrine was one of tolerance of dissent and even of other religions In consequence its leanings were towards political secularism—the separation of the church and the state, equality for all religious beliefs in political matters By long tradition the leading countries of Europe were closely connected with religious establishment The English monarch was and is the head of the Anglican Church which was the established church of the country France proudly claimed to be the eldest daughter of the Catholic Church, as its monarchs had been in the past the Most Christian Majesties and the eldest sons of the Church The liberal trend towards disestablishment and secularism was, therefore, something radical if not revolutionary

A refusal to accept philosophical absolutism or dogmas as binding on society is another aspect of liberalism which deserves emphasis With the development of the view that the objective of politics was the welfare of the people, the idea of conformity with dogmas as the end of social activity began to lose its hold When Charles Darwin promulgated his far reaching theory of evolution—indeed one of the dividing lines of modern thought—liberalism gained a philosophy which had tremendous influence on its social thinking It is difficult today to realise the intensity of the struggle between the dogmatists and the advocates of Darwin's theory of evolution The victory of the latter changed for ever the modern world's approach to social problems Society and its institutions were also seen as subject to evolution and that while there may be comparatively permanent values, institutions and laws and social groupings were as much subject to change as other things in nature In this sense the publication of Darwin's *Origin of Species* is one of the major events contributing to the development of liberalism, which provided it with a philosophic base at once popular, scientific and progressive

The acceptance of evolution as the social doctrine of liberalism, brought it nearly into conflict with the church The *Syllabus* of 1864 by which the Holy See denounced liberal thought found its greatest justification in the attack on dogmas and unchanging morals for which the church stood at all times

Another significant feature of liberalism was the belief that society can be indefinitely improved through the application of organised intelligence and reason to social affairs This was the faith of the great leaders of the Enlightenment This is what the Great Revolution attempted to do The reaction that followed was unable to wipe out this belief wholly In fact the great legislative reforms that Bentham inspired, though they were more corrective of past abuses and did not perhaps claim to build society anew, showed for the first time what legislation could do in a constructive way. We have seen that one of the main characteristics of liberalism was the belief in infinite progress. How was this progress to be achieved ? Legislation as the application of organised intelligence seemed to the liberal thinkers the right way to achieve this end. The contradiction involved in entrusting the state with the control of social forces, and at the same time holding to the rights of the individual as against the state as a dogma, was perhaps obscured by Bentham's formula of the greatest good of the greatest number. In any case the dependence on legislation as an instrument of social reform and consequently of progress was one of the main features of liberalism. In fact the corpus of legislation passed between 1830 and 1914 is perhaps larger than at all previous times combined. Legislation became one of the main activities of government. The fundamental contradiction between the individualistic view of society which in the case of a thinker like Herbert Spencer went to the extent of claiming that the law abiding individual had the right of ignoring the state, and the doctrine that held that it was the duty of the state to reorganise society through legislation will be dealt with later. The contradiction is inherent in liberalism. It arises out of the incompatibility between the idea that the state is a danger to the individual's freedom and the view which holds that through intelligent direction human society could be directed to a better end

Another major strand in liberal thought is the conviction that both individually and collectively it is possible to take a general view, above and beyond vested interests and class considerations Early in life Bentham had postulated the theory of Sinister Interests overriding what was obviously good At mid century Karl Marx was to postulate the theory that class interests dominate all political thinking, that all thinking is in fact socially conditioned From these points of view it naturally follows that an objective view of social welfare affecting all classes is beyond the capacity of any individual or group The liberal doctrine was exactly the opposite of this While the liberal view did not deny the existence of self interest and class motivation in political action, it firmly held that both individually and collectively men are endowed with qualities which enable them to look beyond selfish or class interests The possibility of an objective view of social and political action is one of the postulates of liberalism

The liberal view of the state, based as it was on social contract, deprecated force as its foundation Moral suasion was its instrument Discussion and debate were its methods of arriving at decisions

It is significant that the three main countries in which liberalism developed as a doctrine, and was invested with authority, England, France and U S A , were not only democracies but endowed with representative institutions which decided policy and legislation Apart from parliamentary discussions and debates liberalism attached importance to public opinion In fact everywhere, as Dicey points out in his work *Legislation And Public Opinion in the Nineteenth Century,* legislation on important issues always followed their victory with the general public The liberal era was therefore the great period of public agitations, of nationwide demonstrations, of mass meetings, organised newspaper campaigns, and other methods of arousing public opinion It is the method of what Americans call the Great Debate When the issues have been clarified and public view defined, legislation, according to the liberal view, should follow

The liberal approach to law and judicial administration is another significant feature which requires emphasis The American Bill of Rights contains the best enunciation of the liberal point of view It lays down, as we saw, the rights of the people to be "secure in their persons, houses, papers and effects against unreasonable searches and seizures," that they should not be deprived of liberty, life and property without due process of law, etc The immense significance of these rights would only be understood when it is realised that at the time of enactment these rights were in fact enjoyed nowhere, though in theory they were supposed to have been enjoyed in England The English judicial system before the Benthamite reforms in the next century, in spite of the praise bestowed on it by Blackstone was barbarous in its punishments and cumbersome and dilatory in its procedure So temperate a historian as G M Trevelyan in his *English Social History* describes the situation as follows

> "Throughout the (18th) century Parliament went on adding statute after statute to the 'bloody' code of English law enlarging perpetually the long list of offences punishable by death finally they numbered two hundred Not only were horse and sheep stealing and coining capital offences, but stealing in a shop to the value of five shillings and stealing anything privy from the person were it only a handkerchief"

If such was the barbarous nature of the law, the procedure enforced was something unbelievably chaotic In this connection it is not possible to better the description given by Bentham, the great reformer and one of the founding fathers of liberal legal thought

"We will deny justice—says King John—we will sell justice to no man. This was the wicked King John. How does the good King George III? He denies it ninety nine out of a hundred and sells it to the hundredth. Under English law, not to speak of other systems of the sort of commodity called justice is not only sold but being like gunpowder and spirits made of different degrees of strength is sold at different prices suited to the packet of so many different classes of customers."

So far as procedure under the law prevalent in the 18th century, Bentham had the following to say:

"When an action is brought against a man how do you think they contrive to give him notice to defend himself? Sometimes he is told he is in jail; sometimes that he is walking up and down the country in company with a vagabond of the name of Doe, though all the while he is sitting quietly by his own fireside."

That all this was not wholly a caricature of what existed may be seen from the fact that in 1801 a boy of 12 was hanged for stealing a spoon. In 1786, one Phoebe Harris was burnt alive for coining. There were by no means exceptions. Such was the state of judicial administration in England. In America, the leader of the Hudson Valley agitation against landlords in 1776 was sentenced to be hanged, disembowelled and otherwise mutilated On the continent in some respect it was worse, as even the right to judicial equality or freedom from arbitrary punishment was denied to the people Napoleon to his everlasting credit it must be said, endowed France with a liberal civilised and humane code which soon became the model for other European countries But in England serious legal reforms started only when after the great period of reaction following Waterloo liberalism came to be widely accepted

The liberal attitude to law was that it should be humane and that it should reflect the moral opinion and the sense of justice of the community Social improvements and progress through the instrumentality of legislation is a later doctrine which liberalism accepted at the time of its authority That justice should be independent and that the rule of law should prevail against the arbitrary decisions of the executive were among the first accepted canons of liberalism

These broadly constituted the corpus of liberal principles But it would be an error to think that they were all formulated at the same time and constituted a uniform political programme In fact three periods could be clearly marked in which liberal theory came to be thought out and formulated

The first period was in the seventies of the 18th century but owing to the extravagances of the French Revolution and the Great Fear created by it, the doctrines of the Enlightenment found practical expression only in the United States In Europe this first period of liberalism begins really in 1830 and extends to 1867 With the new Reform Bill of 1867, the Education Act of 1870 in England and the establishment of the Third Republic in France, liberalism enters on its second and more constructive stage The period after 1905 constitutes the third phase when for reasons which we shall analyse later liberalism itself undergoes a transformation which in the next decade leads to its disappearance as a political philosophy

In the first period the doctrines, apart from those relating to legal reforms, were theoretical and vague The right of the citizen was asserted It was vaguely hoped that his condition could in every way be bettered if he had wise laws and good government The main achievements of the first period were the reform of existing institutions and modification of existing evils, e g the Reform Act, Poor Law administration, etc It also saw the repeal of many differentiating laws like those relating to the Catholics and the Jews From the economic point of view the period was not one of reform We shall be making a great mistake if we think that at this period such rights, which we consider elementary to the spirit of liberalism as freedom of association, were generally accepted The following instance may show what the situation was In the winter of 1830, some field labourers marched on to London for pressing their modest wage demand of half a crown a day The consequence of this assembly is thus described by Trevelyan 'The revenge taken by the judges was terrible, three of the rioters were unjustly hanged and four hundred and twenty were torn from their families and transported to Australia as convicts' This is only one example Education of women was not for long considered desirable in any way So far as political rights for women were concerned they were beyond the imagination of the first generation of liberal thinkers

The end of the first period in fact witnessed a growing conflict between liberal thought and practice John Bright, one of the great luminaries of liberalism, argued even at that time in favour of the "right" of children to work for over 11 hours The Supreme Court of America decided in the Dred Scott case that the slave owners had the right to own their slaves In France the so called Liberal Empire was supporting clericalism and quartering French troops in Rome against the

Italian nationalists Napoleon the Third represented in himself some of the major contradictions of liberalism A believer in economic liberalism, a supporter of nationalist claims, a progressive in industrial development, harbour building and construction of railways, one who even foresaw that the Algerian Arabs would one day have to be free, he was also a supporter of clericalism Similar contradictions could be seen in most of the great liberals of this period It is the next phase of liberal development that sought to reconcile these conflicts

II

THE LIBERAL TRANSFORMATION

THE second and more constructive period of liberalism, when its social content found expression in Europe and America can be dated from 1870, but its roots lay farther back in the decades of unrest which culminated in the Chartist movement (1838 57) Though the Chartist movement itself failed and was considered subversive and revolutionary at the time, its main demands like manhood franchise and extension of membership of Parliament and of elective bodies even to those who did not own property came in time to be incorporated in the liberal creed Also the year 1848, the year of revolutions, was not without far reaching effects on liberal thought It is one of the crucial years of European history Apart from unsuccessful revolutions in European capitals, and the dramatic close of Metternich's long domination over continental politics, 1848 was made notable by the Communist Manifesto of Marx A significant but forgotten manifestation of liberalism in that year was the convening of an all German parliament at Frankfurt, which formulated, on the basis of unexceptionable liberal doctrines, a constitution for a unified Germany From the liberal point of view the frustrated revolution of 1848 was particularly significant as the popular ideas behind the discontent became the official policy of the liberalism of the next period

The period was also preceded by a great intellectual activity which helped to shape liberal thought In France they were again formulating vast systems expressing great hopes, Fourier, Saint Simon and Proudhon were giving expression to new political theories Lamartine and Victor Hugo were combining romanticism with political liberalism A distinguished gallaxy of historians, among whom may be mentioned two important political leaders, Guizot and Thiers, and which included Edgar Quinet and Michelet, provided a historic basis for new thinking Belief in science and progress had become popular again in France In England this great intellectual revival which provided the background for liberalism was notable in many different fields, science, political thinking and history Darwin's *Origin of Species* was of course epoch-making and provided liberal thought with a scientific basis for its evolutionary approach to social problems John Stuart Mill's essays on "Liberty", "Representative Government" and on "The Subjection of Women" (1869) were notable landmarks in liberal thinking Lecky's *History of Rationalism* and Buckles' *History of Civilisation* (1857) expressed the growing optimism of the age

With the Reform Bill of 1867 the new era of liberalism may be said to have started on its astonishing career which within a period of thirty years transformed western society and also began to spread its beneficent rays to other parts of the world Its political social and economic content deserves careful analysis as it was largely guided by purposive creative action and not merely by the idea of correcting abuses as in the earlier period

Politically the significant fact is the changing conception of the state Up to this period there was an unstated identification of the state with property-owning classes Even the Reform Act of 1832 did not materially change this situation as it limited the franchise to property holders Young T B Macaulay, a true liberal, far in advance of his time, speaking in the House of Commons on the Reform Bill of 1832 deplored that the condition of the working classes had not progressed sufficiently for them to be entrusted with the right of electing members of the legislature though he pointed out that in the U S A universal manhood suffrage (subject of course to the exclusion of slaves) existed "without producing any very frightful consequences' After emphasising the backward conditions of the labouring classes in England he came to the conclusion that it is clearly "expedient that in a country like this, the thought of suffrage should depend upon a pecuniary qualification" Forty five years later in 1867 it was the Tory Prime Minister Disraeli who declared, speaking again in the House of Commons on Franchise and Reform, that no measure of Parliamentary Reform could be deemed satisfactory which did not remedy the great fault of the Act of 1832, "that of denying to give a share of representation to the working classes' How far the doctrine of liberalism had penetrated political thinking may be judged from the fact that this highly significant broadening of franchise and its justification came from a Tory Prime Minister Soon in fact manhood suffrage came to be accepted as the liberal doctrine though adult suffrage including votes to women came only much later

The extension of the concept of the state to include the totality of its membership, men and women, though given effect to fully only after the eclipse of liberalism following the first Great War, was also a liberal idea Adult franchise was the law in America though negro slaves and American Indians who paid no tax were excluded from franchise By the 15th amendment of 1870 it was however provided in law "that the right of the citizens of the United States to vote shall not be denied or abridged by the United States or by any State on account of race colour or previous condition of servitude " Though legally the full rights of citizenship and suffrage were thus extended to the Negroes in 1870 it is, however, undeniable that in many states the exercise of this franchise was denied or limited by various technically legal methods In France the liberal principle of the state being identified with the people (though women were excluded here also) was carried to its logical limit of direct consultation with the people (plebiscite) by Napoleon III The gradual extension of the concept of the state to cover the entire male population may therefore be considered as a major achievement of liberalism in the 19th century

Liberalism was however basically the creed of the middle classes who claimed to be the real representatives of the people, as industry, commerce, liberal professions and intellectual activity—in fact all aspects of the expression of national energy—were concentrated in their hands Writers, poets, artists, scientists and all others who contributed to the culture of the period came from the middle classes A Toulouse Lautrec or Isle d Adam, a duc de Broglie or a Byron or a Balfour was an exception In the financial industrial and commercial fields their supremacy was absolute Though in England, until the end of the century, Cabinets were weighted by members of the House of Lords, excepting of course the leading Prime Ministers, Peel, Palmerston (an Irish Peer who sat in the Commons), Gladstone and Disraeli, Parliament was dominated by the middle classes during this period, the land owning gentry who represented the country seats was giving way slowly to the tide of urban representation In France, as early as 1830, aristocracy had practically disappeared from the political stage The July monarchy was almost by definition a bourgeois regime Though in the Second Empire dukes and counts sat in cabinets and seats of power, it was an imitation aristocracy whose coronets and ermines could not conceal its middle class origin With the Third Republic the middle classes were firmly in the saddle Broadly this was the position also in Italy In Germany alone, of the major European states, the landed aristocracy continued to exercise political power in the liberal era, though even here the phenomenal growth of industry and commerce developed a new class whose influence was fast growing and before the end of the century the industrial classes of the Rhineland and the commercial magnates of the Hanseatic ports had become the real wielders of power

The middle class however did not form a closed society any where It was being regularly recruited and enlarged from both below and from above. The immense strides which industry and commerce were making in this period helped to create new classes not only of rich people, but of the intermediate class of managers and other higher paid employees who became the backbone of the new life In France and America the development of the new classes was even more visible than in England America became, in the period between the civil war and the first world war, the great emigrant society in which the poor and the persecuted from everywhere began to congregate, the Irish, the Italians, the Poles, Central Europeans of all races invaded the inheritance of the Boston Brahmins and the earlier colonisers The new emigrants came as poor people—"Cattle Irish", emigrants who fled from the potato famines which disgraced British rule in Ireland at this period In the next generation a large percentage of this group became "lace curtain" Irish who in the third generation climbed to the higher rungs of the ladder in industry, intellectual life and political leadership Broadly this was true of most emigrant people not only the Irish, but the Italians, the Germans, the Poles and the Czechs The emergence of a new middle class from out of these poor emigrants is perhaps the most striking phenomenon in American social history of the second half of 19th century Their influence was rapidly growing at this period

The fact that the middle classes did not constitute a closed group had a significant result The extension of the concept of the nation to include all classes came naturally to them The nobility and the land owning classes everywhere have at all times considered themselves as constituting the nation and liberty and rights as something to which they were specially entitled The rise of the middle classes helped to change this idea

The social content of liberalism, though it was being broadened, was determined by a few major ideas national education, economic freedom and opportunity for women, secularism in social and educational policies and the organisation of trade unions to safeguard the interests of labour These formed the main elements of the social policies of the period In the economic sphere, liberalism in this era of its greatest development, stood for the unrestricted operation of private enterprise and free trade, in short for the principle of *laissez faire* As it was a period of territorial expansion when the almost inexhaustible markets of Asia seemed to be opening up for the products of Europe, free trade and open competition in world markets seemed to be self-evident truths to the great industrialists, merchant companies and banks which controlled the economic life of the mercantile nations of

Europe In any case within a period of thirty years the social programme of liberalism changed the face of western Europe and the United States while the dynamism of the new industrial and economic programmes inspired by liberalism gave rise to a prosperity unprecedented in history

Of the social content of liberalism, its attitude to education may be considered first All civilisations recognised and emphasised the importance of education The scribe was honoured and respected among ancient Egyptians Education was highly prized among the Hindus The Chinese honoured the scholar The prophet Mohammed enjoined his followers to seek knowledge even in far off countries Great universities and some organisations on a national scale for affording education existed in all civilised communities But everywhere education was left either to religious organisations like *mutts* and monasteries, temples and mosques or to private endowment At no time before the liberal experiment was the provision of education considered a duty of the state In 1833 in England after a great deal of argument a paltry sum of twenty thousand pounds annually was provided towards school buildings of various voluntary organisations As Trevelyan says, 'To distribute this pittance an educational committee of the Privy Council was set up, with a permanent secretary and a system of inspection of the State-aided schools Such was the humble origin of the Board of Education "

But even this system of limited aid did not mean the acceptance of state responsibility for education Far from this being the case there was the general feeling that education of what was called the lower classes would lead to interference with the supply of labour This was even more pronounced in America Speaking of the demand for the extension of state supported schools, Merle Custi, in his *Growth of American Thought*, explaining the opposition of men of power and substance to such schemes says. 'They themselves felt satisfied with the training their children received in private schools, if the poor did not and could not provide schooling for their offspring, the fault must be laid at the door of their own shiftlessness and incompetency Free school laws, it was argued, merely filled the bellies and covered the backs of the indigent at the expense of the tax payer To provide free schools for the less well to do would result in the loss of their self respect and initiative it would in brief pauperize them " Some argued that free public schools must be opposed on the ground that they would provide education to those "who were better suited to their station without it" This was not very different from the alleged Brahmin attitude towards educated Sudras

The idea that every man had a right to education which farseeing liberal thinkers like Lord Brougham had put forward did not receive wide acceptance either in England or in America or in France at this time A leading spokesman of industrialists in America in the middle of the last century, Edward Everett, in opposing this demand for free education, declared "you might as well argue that the state must pay his tailor" But with the growth of liberal sentiment this attitude was fast changing Political leaders like Horace Mann had popularised the doctrine that the provision of education was the first concern of the state In his famous fourth of July oration Mann asked that "for every acre of land bestowed upon an academy, a province should have been granted to common schools The noblest public edifices", he added, "the most splendid galleries of art, theatres, gardens, monuments should all have been deemed a reproach to any people while there was a child among them without ample and improved method and means of education"

In the sixties, opinion began to veer round to the view, as Lincoln put it, that education is the most important activity that a people can be engaged in In England, Foster's Act provided free and compulsory primary education for all children upto the age of eleven This, as we can now see, was a revolutionary step Side by side with this, the facilities for higher education also were thrown open to all Oxford and Cambridge which had previously been confined to members of the Anglican church were thrown open to all in 1871 without reference to religious belief This was the result of a strenuous fight "of an academic liberal party of great intellectual distinction' The London University which had been founded in 1827 to provide for non conformists and for the new classes became a major factor in intellectual life at this period

The fight for a secular conception of state, which provided not only for freedom of conscience and for toleration of dissent but for the elimination of favoured treatment for those who followed a particular sect or religion, was an essential aspect of the growth of liberalism It was a part of the theory of enlightenment in the 18th century and found early realisation in the United States The Bill of Rights specially emphasised this but in European states with long traditions of established churches, persecution of dissent, vested interests of establishments in finances (tithes), education and power, it was no easy matter to get the principle of secularism accepted The alliance between the altar and the throne, and where the throne had been discarded as in France, with the reactionary elements of society, was a most notorious fact which could not easily be broken In England the growth of non conformist *communities powerful in many fields* but nourishing a sense of complaint about the privileged position accorded to the Church of England and the princely salaries amenities and special status provided at public expenses to the higher dignitaries of the Anglican church constituted a political problem The monarch being the head of the church made any attack on it sound faintly seditious

The extent of this integral relationship between the Anglican church and English institutions before the rise of liberalism to full power in the 1860 s may be judged from the following facts As we have already noticed under Lord Hardwicke s Act of 1753 no one could be legally married in England except in an Anglican church (This was repealed in 1836) No one could matriculate at Oxford or graduate in Cambridge without signing the 39 articles of the Anglican creed till the Test Act of 1871 Anglican Bishops sat in the House of Lords There were a number of posts of the highest importance which were understood to be open only to those who professed the Anglican creed The feeling that the English nation and the Anglican church were to be equated though it was slowly weakening was still held widely in orthodox circles to such an extent that the mere re establishment of a catholic hierarchy in England (1850) was greeted with popular outburst "against papal aggression on England' The process of secularisation was, therefore, slow but in the three decades that constituted the high water mark of liberal thought in England, the state accepted the ideas of secularism while still maintaining in form its association with the Anglican church Balfour's Education Act of 1902 brought the church schools under the control of local authorities to a large extent A curious incident which shows how even in the liberal age it was difficult for people in authority to be tolerant when it came to religious matters, is illustrated by the famous Bradlaugh case Charles Bradlaugh was one of the leading radicals of the time, a friend of all progressive causes and a public figure of considerable importance, but he was an atheist When elected to the House of Commons he refused to take his oath on the Bible but offered to make an affirmation The Commons refused him permission to do so and he was thus deprived of his right to take his seat His seat was declared vacant He was re elected but again the majority in the Commons was adamant It was only after much trouble that Bradlaugh was allowed to take his seat after a simple affirmation

If in England the struggle for secularism was weighted in favour of the church by its relationship with the monarchy, in France the alliance between the altar and the throne was deeply imbedded in the political tradition and found its reflection even under the Republic. The clerical policy of Napoleon III and the support that the church gave to him had alienated French liberal opinion even before the Third Republic was established. When the Third Republic was stabilised after a short period of reaction, its historical inheritance as the successor of the two revolutions, apart from the prejudices created against the church by its alliance with the Extreme Right, led to a wave of anti-clerical feeling in radical circles. The most important step in this movement was the famous educational code of Jules Ferry which deprived unauthorised congregations like the Jesuits the right to teach. Ferry was a passionate advocate of lay morality who went to the extent of suppressing religious teaching in state schools. In France it was thus an open fight, the church facing undaunted the massed authority of the state. So bitter was the church's feeling against secularism that Monseigneur Dupanloup preferred to resign from the French Academy than be a colleague of the positivist Littre. But the church's position was greatly weakened by its alliance with the reactionary forces, and the famous Dreyfus case, in which the advocates of a secular state mobilised their strength and carried on a prolonged struggle against the massed forces of the right, the church, the army and the nobility, to ultimate victory constituted a watershed in modern French history

From the beginning of the 20th century there has never been any serious questioning of the secular character of the liberal state Where the establishment exists as in England, or where the church continues to be influential as in France, there is no question either of any intolerance of dissent or a favoured political position for the followers of any particular sect In England this position was made easier in spite of the monarch being the head of the established church by the fact that the overseas dominions contained large numbers of the followers of all the religions of the world At the height of its greatness as a liberal nation, the British Empire contained more Muslims than any other country, included the vast majority of Hindus and counted millions of Buddhists in its population, not to speak of the large number of catholics in Ireland, Canada and Australia Whatever the legal position, British monarchy had in fact to uphold a liberal and secular attitude in politics

Another major plank in the social platform of liberalism related to the position of women At the beginning of the 19th century the position of women was something which would seem unbelievable today The great European countries of France,

Germany, Italy and England produced in recent centuries many women of outstanding intelligence and political influence In France the great salons of the 18th century show how pervading was the influence of women In England the famous Georgiana, Duchess of Devonshire, was no doubt an exception but not a few had shown that they could break through the shackles that society imposed upon them It is indeed undeniable that the middle period of the 18th century in Europe was dominated by three women, Catherine the Great of Russia, Maria Theresa of the Habsburgs and Madame de Pompadour But the legal rights of women were indeed limited Politically they had no rights, economically they were dependent, socially they were not allowed any active participation in professions In education also they were differentiated against Mary Wollencroft's *Vindication of the Rights of Women* (1792) is perhaps the first clear and unequivocal statement of women's claims and yet there is an interval of 78 years between that book and Mill's great work on the subjection of women If in fact the position of women underwent considerable modification during this period it is well to remember that this was mainly a result of the penetration of liberal ideas The most notable change was in relation to property Till the Married Woman's Property Act late in Queen Victoria's reign, a woman's property became a husband's at marriage in curious contrast, as the social historian of England points out, to the words of the marriage service when the man was made to say "with all my worldly goods I thee endow". Though this was the position of the married women the growth of industries and the consequent employment of women as factory hands altered the economic position of unmarried women The economic independence achieved by the women factory workers created in fact a minor social revolution

The prejudice against women in the educational field was very widespread It was only in 1865 that girls were permitted to sit for Cambridge local examination Though colleges were established at Oxford and Cambridge some time later, and women were allowed to sit for examinations, they were not admitted to degrees till after the first Great War

In this sphere, more than in most others, the penetration of liberal ideas was slow Only a small group of people in the most advanced countries were prepared to accept the equality of men and women Most shared Tennyson's view expressed in the line in "Locksley Hall" that "woman is unto man as is water unto wine" The prejudice went to such an extent that in 1841 the world anti-slavery convention in London refused to admit American women delegates This led to the strange result that two of them, Lucretia Mott and Elizabeth Stanton, decided to launch a women's rights movement on their return to America Their programme was contained in a Declaration of Sentiment (1848), which in phraseology was reminiscent of the Declaration of Independence, indicted man of his tyrannies over women

Though it took a considerable time before women gained political rights, the movement for their social and occupational freedom achieved success before the end of the century. The liberal point of view with regard to children and young people may also be alluded to here. Before the rise of liberalism it was never considered that the state had any interest in children at all. It was held to be exclusively a matter for the family, the parents or other relations. It was only when the factories began to employ child labour on a large scale, for long hours and low wages, that national conscience was, in some degree, aroused to the scandal. And yet John Bright, that shining light of liberal Manchester, opposed a law proposing to reduce the hours of work to 10 as interfering with the freedom of the individual. The employment of children brought money to the parents' pockets and consequently the labouring classes were not greatly in favour of the abolition of child labour. Public opinion was however greatly aroused not so much by popular agitation as by the writings of that new prophet of liberalism, Dickens, whose *Oliver Twist* deserves to be placed in the category of books which more than public agitations have awakened the conscience of men. Effective protection of children from exploitation came however only with the Education Act which made attendance at schools compulsory and thereby prevented their employment in factories It is worth mentioning in this connection that in America the situation continued to be unsatisfactory for quite a long time afterwards In the Bailey Case the Supreme Court struck down an attempt to prohibit child labour In the Adkins Case it struck down a District of Columbia law fixing minimum wage for women and children

The liberal attitude towards labour was in the beginning vitiated by a contradiction The first principle of liberalism was individual liberty It also believed in *laissez faire* as the best policy in economic matters Equally, liberalism claimed to be the voice of industrial advancement The new liberal world seemed to emerge through industrialism and free trade and Cobden and Bright appeared to be the prophets of the new era A combination of these doctrines, individualism, *laissez-faire* and industrial development argued inevitably against any policy of protection for labour. The phrase in common use was the "labour market".

Was not an individual entitled to sell his labour in the free market? To this question the first generation of liberals had no reply In fact when factory legislation came to a head in the period between 1845–1847 it found liberal opinion very much divided When so moderate a measure as the Ten Hours Bill came up for voting, Cobden and Bright voted against it It is not our purpose here to trace the growth of the measures for the protection of labour and for the right of workers to better wages, healthier conditions, insurance, old age pension, etc which form a major chapter in the social history of all the progressive countries of the modern world Though the liberal attitude to these issues was hesitant and wavering to start with on the ground of interference with individual freedom the growth of social conscience in the later half of the period led to what in effect was a revolution in economic history In the pre-liberal era up to 1825 combinations of workers had been considered seditious When that law was repealed, trade unionism began to grow and the claims of labour for higher wages and better conditions became more and more insistant But the courts held (1867) that trade unions, being in restraint of trade, were illegal associations By this time liberal opinion had cast off its earlier doubts and Gladstone's Act (1871) restored the legal position of the unions

After this the trade unions became one of the factors in British public life, organising both skilled and unskilled labour and gradually moving into the political arena The fight however was not over The Taffe Vale decision in 1901 declared strikes illegal but by this time the political power of labour had become so great that the decision had to be legislatively amended

Briefly it may be said that the liberal era witnessed three major changes in regard to the working classes, apart from their accession to political suffrage In the first place factory acts were enacted laying down the basic conditions under which work was to be carried on The second related to the work itself the limitation of hours, special conditions for women and children, etc The third was the gradual legalisation of trade unions and their activities, and action for the protection of workers interests Cumulatively it led to a social transformation which is difficult to parallel at any other period of history

Nor was this confined to England In France, Germany and to a lesser extent in Italy, the changes that came about in this field were equally remarkable

There are many other facets of liberal thought which the social, political or economic historian cannot fail to note Basically liberalism came to be based on reform and relativism It emphasised the right of judgment and moral censure, and it is a fact to be noted and emphasised that though paradoxical to some extent, the liberal historians of the period were not afraid to pronounce judgements or give praise and blame according to the moral values they preached Their interpretation of history was no doubt from a liberal point of view, it was sometimes narrow, sometimes prejudiced but it never hesitated to pronounce moral values on periods, unlike Ranke who declared pompously that God held every age equally dear to him

Further it is significant that the period of liberal predominance witnessed the growth of an international conscience The Putemayo atrocities, the scandals of Belgian Congo, the Armenian massacres and other international incidents aroused widespread protest Nor were these limited to conditions for which other people were responsible Dickens' exposure of conditions in England moved public opinion deeply So did Balzac and Zola by their descriptions arouse in France a passion for reform In fact liberalism in its great period may be said to have provided humanity with a new conscience.

III

THE WEAKNESS OF LIBERALISM

IN THE first decade of the twentieth century liberalism had reached the high water mark of its influence and was betraying signs of being corroded by other doctrines and modified by the unsuspected implications of the developments which had originated under its own influence In this last period western Europe (outside Spain and Portugal) and, in America, U S A and Canada, had become transformed in their social, economic and political life by the influence of liberal doctrine To many people this statement may seem strange in respect especially of Germany and Italy But a moment's consideration will show that prejudices apart, prejudices created by later events, Imperial Germany from 1870 to 1914, despite the trappings of the Prussian monarchy and the emphasis placed on its armed forces, was essentially a liberal state It is true the Emperor William II strutted about in uniforms, made tactless speeches, and seemed to challenge his neighbours But as against these antics may be remembered the fact, often forgotten now, that in Imperial Germany the Reichstag was elected on universal franchise, that there was complete freedom in universities, that labour legislation was more advanced than in most countries and that national insurance was the official policy in Germany long before it was thought of in England When we recall that in German Parliament Karl Liebknecht and Rosa Luxemburg were free to oppose the regime and that before the war the *Vorward* the socialist paper, was an outspoken critic of the regime, that human rights were not interfered with by government, the idea that Imperial Germany was a monarchical version of the Nazi regime, outside the liberal traditions of Europe, would be found to be a prejudice surviving from the period of the first Great War

In Italy the liberal tradition was no less pronounced though in its operation it was less effective than in Germany The northern states, Denmark, Norway and Sweden, in an unspectacular way accepted and put into effect the ideas of liberalism more thoroughly than perhaps all other states of Europe Also at this time in areas outside Europe and America, liberal ideas began to take root The rays of enlightenment had reached India early Ram Mohan Roy was in correspondence with many advanced thinkers in Europe and his writings show clearly the influence of European liberal thought But it was only in the period following the Great Rebellion (1857) that liberalism as a political philosophy gained the adherence of Indian intellectuals

At the time when the area of its influence was at its widest, unsuspected weaknesses began to manifest themselves in liberal societies The main conceptions of liberalism such as liberty, equality, the rights of the individual and freedom of speech seemed inadequate to the changed conditions of society In the 18th century when in Europe kings could detain any body in jail and nobles like Chevalier de Rohan could beat up men like Voltaire in streets without legal remedy, personal liberty was a very real problem But in the liberal states where the rights of the individual against arbitrary arrests etc were fully secured the definition of liberty as non interference with the person of individual was obviously inadequate Did this precious liberty include, as John Bright evidently held the right of boys and girls of tender age to be employed in factories? Was individual liberty being infringed when trade unions were bargaining collectively or engaging themselves in peaceful picketing? Freedom liberty and such other ideas clearly required a new interpretation

Also liberalism seemed to oversimplify issues The basic ideas of liberal thought which struck early nineteenth century as something new and idealistic lost much of their sheen through use and familiarity Also, it was clear that liberalism was a philosophy of prosperity The Marxian analysis of social and economic problems was opening the eyes of the intellectuals to many of the problems which were created by the very success of liberalism The recurring problem of unemployment, the large scale creation of slums around fast growing industrial areas, the problems of housing, the obviously unjust distribution of wealth and many other factors which distinguished the liberal societies at the end of the 19th century showed clearly that the doctrine of free enterprise, open markets, individual initiative, etc on which the liberal society had been built up created many new problems, for which the original doctrines of liberalism seemed to provide no remedy Automatic progress in the sense of greater and greater production of material goods seemed to have been achieved, but the price that society had to pay for this unlimited faith in *laissez-faire* began to awaken the conscience of the community The critics of the Left inspired by Marxian thinking did not fail to point out that the social or economic principles "which Victorian Englishmen accepted as basic and eternal were but the interests of one particular island development and the truths which they so dogmatically bound upon themselves and upon others and in the name of which they felt justified in acting as they did were their own pressing economic and political needs and claims masquerading as individual truths "[1] The Tracts of the Fabian Society, to mention only the mildest and most constructive of these approaches, turned the searchlight on many of the economic and social conceptions which liberalism had for long considered to be axiomatic and showed them up to be inadequate for the requirements of the time

New problems required new solutions The growth of organised labour as a major power and a growing interest in the state was something which liberalism did not and could not have foreseen But this was the great development of the middle period between 1870 and 1906 The rise of the working classes and their organisation as a force capable of bringing pressure was something which passed the understanding of liberal thinkers When later the workers organised their own political party claiming the allegiance of millions it appeared to many genuine liberals a threat to the doctrine of the state itself It was denounced as the revolt of the masses, to use the words of Ortega Y Gasset The liberal theory of the state recognised no intermediate loyalties logically nothing stood between the individual and the state The intermediate allegiance towards Guilds, Churches, etc were considered to be a medieval conception which limited the liberty of the individual no less than it restricted the authority

[1] *Berlin Historical Inevitability* p 43

of the state The growth of the major trade unions, and naturally of the parallel employers' organisations, demonstrated clearly the weakness of the liberal conception of the state The intermediate allegiances returned again as a major factor in political life strangely enough by the legislation promoted by the new liberals, as for example wheu they struck down by legislative action the decision in the Taff Vale case and legalised the immunities of the trade unions and erected them into a privileged position Broadly the doctrine that the straight line of human evolution was from status to contract, which liberalism had accepted almost as an axiom, seemed to become increasingly unrelated to facts when collective bargaining took the place of free sale of labour This was one of the major developments which undermined the conceptions of the liberal state

Two other contradictions began to manifest themselves in liberalism The first was its attitude towards imperialism and the second towards solution by state activity of the social problems that the great liberal transformation had created Obviously the basic doctrines of liberalism, liberty, equality, fraternity, individualism, freedom of thought, expression, etc could not approve of the domination of one nation over another It is indeed difficult to reconcile either the doctrines or practices of imperialism with the basic conceptions of liberal thought And yet it is the period of unchallenged liberal authority which witnessed the greatest expansion of imperialism over Asia and Africa To some extent it was a consequence of free enterprise and search for free markets, to a greater extent it was the result of planned governmental action arising out of the belief that control of the resources of these areas would contribute to the strength of the mother country, as also that the possession of an empire would add to its prestige and greatness During the great days of liberalism, Britain undertook the direct administration of India, conquered and annexed Burma, established an all pervading authority over Chinese Empire, created a *de facto* protectorate over Egypt, took over the Sudan and brought large areas of Africa under her control France, the other great liberal power, was not to be beaten at this game The states of Indo China constituted France s empire in the East and Algeria Tunis and later Morocco came under her occupation or protectorate An immense area of Africa was added to the French Empire, all this at a time when the principles of liberalism were being proclaimed from house tops Nor was America less aggressive in her policy of territorial expansion A distinguished American historian, Van Alstyne, has demonstrated that contrary to popular belief, and in spite of her professions of liberalism, the United States was consciously following an imperialist policy till the first Great War when it emerged as one of the satiated powers Imperialism was in fact one of the major aspects of the period from which no great nation was exempt

Even a casual examination would show how the ideas on which imperialism was based were incompatible with the basic ideals of liberalism To conquer and hold a country and to keep its people in subjugation could not but be considered as denying the rights of liberty, equality and fraternity Subjection is the opposite of liberty and imperial rule, whatever it may claim as its objective, frankly denied liberty as a current fact to the people it held in subjection The denial of liberty is in fact the basis of imperialism So far as equality was concerned the advocates of imperial rule proceeded on the assumption that the natives were of an inferior breed This is well known and too recent a fact to need any proof The concept of the white man's burden implied that the non whites, over whom white men ruled, could not be considered their equals in any matter Once the question of subordination of a people became a fact, and racial inferiority a matter of dogma, there was of course no question of fraternity

The contradiction between the doctrines of liberalism and the practice of imperialism was however not limited to their general ideas The conditions of imperial rule rendered it impossible to give effect to the programmes of social and economic developments that liberalism carried out in metropolitan countries Social betterment through legislation was never seriously attempted in any colonial area The urge for reorganising society on liberal principles was not there, no doubt partly because it was felt that such reforms may give rise to discontent but partly also because the evils which such legislation was meant to remedy did not directly touch the alien rulers of the country There was also the lurking fear that if these subject communities were launched on the path of progress the days of imperial rule would be numbered In the later stages of imperial domination therefore the doctrine in authority was that of indirect rule as in Nigeria which was recommended first on the ground of cheapness and secondly as not giving rise to progressive social movements

Economically also the doctrines of imperialism conflicted with those associated with liberal thought In all the colonies and protectorates under imperial rule the growth of industry was discouraged as the broad interest of the metropolitan countries was to keep the areas under their domination as sources for the production of cheap raw materials and minerals for their own industries and as closed or at least reserved markets for their industrial goods Industrialisation which was one of the creeds of liberalism was considered good only for the metropolitan countries The story of the countervailing duty on Indian cotton goods forced on the Government of India by the British Government is perhaps the best illustration of this tendency The Government of India in the interests of revenue decided to impose a small duty on imported cotton goods The British Government in England in the interests of free trade and of Lancashire cotton industry insisted on the Government of India imposing an equivalent countervailing duty on Indian manufactured cotton textiles Lancashire was then notoriously the citadel of liberalism and it was said that there were sixty different reasons for enforcing this countervailing duty, one for each of the 60 members who represented that area in Parliament

A study of the economic policies of imperialism is not germane to our purpose here What is relevant to our discussion is its incompatibility with the theories of liberalism The very fact that upto the date of their independence the colonial areas were in their economic policies tied to their metropolitan countries and their interests were generally subordinated to those of the mother country, would demonstrate this fact clearly

There was at all times a half hearted attempt to reconcile these contradictions On the political plane the liberals pretended at least that the domination which they alleged they had been forced by circumstances to exercise was only for the benefit of the subject peoples whom they were civilising and instructing in the process of self-government, that much against their wishes they were carrying the white man's burden of being the trustees of their less advanced brethren, that they were gradually inculcating in them those principles of freedom and social welfare which had made the imperial nations great, that they were in most cases providing these areas for the first time with beneficent administrations, progressive laws, impartial justice, and further that through the large scale domination of European nations whole continents were living in peace which was the first condition for the growth of civilisation The French believed that their imperialism, even when it involved heavy burdens for the subject races, was a *Mission Civilisatrice* The British believed that the white man's burden they were carrying was for preserving law and order in areas where otherwise chaos would prevail The imperialist interlude in American politics was always talked about a little apologetically by American liberal leaders

However incompatible with liberal principles and however contradictory to liberal ideas, there is no denying the fact that the growth of imperialism was during the period of liberal dominance and has in some ways to be connected with it It is the immense growth of industry and economic power associated with the great era of liberalism that led to the search for the new markets, that considered it to be in the natural course of things that undeveloped areas should be developed by the more advanced countries, that the natives should be put to productive labour, etc It was also considered illiberal and unnatural that backward nations should sit like dogs in the manger and not develop their resources when the liberal advanced nations were prepared to do so for them Thus it should be obvious that this growth of imperialism in the liberal countries was a logical outcome of some aspects of liberal thought whose contradictions were only faintly being realised at the time

It is however but just and fair to say that while imperialism was an outgrowth of liberalism and found some of its strongest advocates among those who professed advanced liberal principles, there was always a body of opinion which realised the dangerous implications of imperialism not so far as they related to the subject people but to the metropolitan country itself The anti-imperialist tradition was a genuine one among the liberals and though powerless to stop what seemed at the time to be an irresistible movement, it bravely fought on in the face of much calumny and misunderstanding It would also not be wholly true to say that the anti imperialist opinion among the liberals was without influence The dissidents were able to introduce liberal strands in the web of imperial administration Legislative codes, educational policies and generally speaking, the elements of the great categories of liberal freedoms of person, thought, etc were introduced in territories under imperial rule Liberal groups at home, conscious of the arbitrary nature of imperial government, performed the functions of the watch dogs of liberty That the gradual modification of the rigours of imperialist domination and the introduction of self governing institutions in the colonies of the liberal powers was, at least to some extent the result of the pressure of liberal opinion may be seen from the fact that imperialist countries with no liberal traditions like Spain and Portugal still continue to hold on to their colonial regimes leading to continued conflicts and upheavals

Also, as we shall show later, the liberal imperialist nations—whatever their internal contradictions—were to some extent responsible for planting the seeds of liberalism in their colonial areas Laws introduced emphasised the principles of equality at least in relation to indigenous populations The system of education established by the colonial rulers in British, French and American areas popularised liberal principles in political, social and economic spheres There was also—subject always to the necessities of imperial security—freedom of thought It is the liberalism of the metropolitan countries that in part was responsible for the growth of liberalism in the colonial and dependent territories

An even more basic contradiction than the growth of imperialism, something which finally overshadowed the liberal concepts and became a leading feature of politics in the post liberal period was the growth of the administering state The theory behind the leviathan state and its relationship to new liberalism, we shall discuss in the next lecture. Here the growth of administration is touched upon only as a characteristic of the last phase of the pre socialist liberalism Administration in England and America, representing a genuine individualist tradition, was for a long time of a limited character In France, the growth of royal power had been in some measure associated with the development of administration especially under Louis XIV, and this tendency became even more marked and finally was institutionalised in the time of Napoleon And yet, though France was different in this respect and the administrative machinery there was more complex and had more authority than in England or America, even France had not become the administrative state that it now is till the period of the great liberal movements

In England the transition may be said to have begun with the introduction of the income tax Its collection and administration required a national civil service The days when England could carry on her administration with a few thousand clerks and a body of amateur magistrates and politicians were gradually drawing to a close The great body of legislation which was being enacted by Parliament required a large body of trained administrators The new civil services recruited through open competitive examination (1870), the long delayed result of the Trevelyan and Northcote's Report, may be considered as the starting point of this extraordinary development which was to lead to a situation when a professor of politics at Oxford could, without causing surprise or evoking protest, describe the Government of England as a parliamentary bureaucracy With the increasing responsibility which Parliament was placing on the administration, the development of a bureaucracy was unavoidable The latter day prophet of liberalism, John Stuart Mill, in his last days had foreseen this He had pleaded in his last writings for a bureaucracy, national and local, which would efficiently enforce social legislation The last two decades of the great liberal experiment preceding the Great War were a commentary on this text

Mill indeed had foreseen that society would have to move forward from liberalism, that while liberal doctrines would have to be permanently incorporated in progressive social tradition their fulfilment would have to come through other ways He had produced a completely new liberal programme, greatly at variance with the original doctrines to which liberalism had attached importance His programme included ' better distribution of wealth by direct taxation, particularly taxes on inheritance, better conditions of life by social legislation enforced by an effective bureaucracy, national and local a complete system of manhood and womanhood suffrage not only for parliament but for the bodies entrusted with local government " That this new programme was greatly influenced by socialism and its realisation was bound to lead to the disappearance of liberalism as a separate political doctrine must have been obvious even at the time

Post Victorian liberalism was indeed an attempt to translate Mill's views into practice From the economic point of view the liberal programme went very near socialism. Taxation of unearned incomes, death and succession duties, high income-tax and other proposals meant to distribute national income on a more equitable basis and to finance such proposals involving social justice, as old age pensions, national housing schemes, etc. showed that the liberalism of the post Victorian age was something new: that in its social and economic conceptions it had travelled far beyond the undiluted liberalism of the past and had taken over some of the socialist ideas.

A weakness which this latter day liberalism developed arose from the change that began to overtake industrial organisation. Free competition on which the liberal economics of the past was based began to disappear with the growth of cartels and monopolies. Even where cartels and monopolies had not succeeded in taking over, evidences of imperfect competition began to manifest itself. Economic power began to be concentrated increasingly in a few hands, undermining in fact some of the basic conceptions of freedom. In the face of this unexpected phenomenon, which in part was the result of the pursuit of the liberal doctrines of free competition and enterprise unhampered by state control, liberalism was divided in mind and ineffective in action. In the United

States the significance of this development was recognised earlier and the Sherman anti trust legislation was the American liberals' answer to this new menace to freedom That the anti trust laws have not succeeded in halting the process of concentration of industrial power is now recognised, but at least an attempt was made in America to limit the growth of industrial monopolies But in England and France liberal thought does not seem to have considered this development a serious menace to liberty, though it was clear that the concentration of industrial and commercial power in the hands of a few mammoth organisations gave a new, different and not altogether desirable meaning to old slogan of *laissez faire*

It is not only the conception of *laissez faire* whose meaning came to be distorted in later liberalism Freedom of the press—as representing opinion—was one of the cherished ideals of the past In the post Victorian era the emergence of Lord Northcliffe as the first Napoleon of the press to be followed soon by other minor dictators gave even to this valued privilege a distorted meaning and greatly diminished its value Freedom of the press was no longer to be interpreted as the right of independent minds to express their views freely on matters of public importance, but as the claim of newspaper proprietors themselves financial or industrial magnates, to manipulate public opinion Journalism had travelled far from the days of Wilks *North Briton* which defied George III, or Rocheforts' *Lantern* produced cladestinely to attack the policies of Napoleon III The newspapers at the beginning of the century were great industrial undertakings involving immense investment and very complicated organisation for production and distribution In America this development produced the strange and powerful figure of Randolph Hearst who owned a powerful chain of newspapers from coast to coast whose policy in many national matters represented his personal views The freedom of the press so far as he and others like him were concerned was the right to shout the views of the owner through a hundred megaphones There was no question of freedom for the editor, the commentator or the wandering reporter The position was not very different in England where after Northcliffe the freedom of the press became the freedom of the proprietor to propagate his views to the public

It may however be recognised that in all liberal countries the tradition of an independent press, free from the domination of what Bentham would have called the Sinister Interests, continued to have considerable influence

Again this phenomenon, it should be remembered, was the result—unexpected and no doubt unwanted—of liberal policies. The system of free and compulsory national education which was a major achievement of liberalism resulted in converting the whole nation into a newspaper reading public. The newspapers which catered to the interest of this new and ever increasing mass of readers achieved circulation of many millions. The production and circulation of papers on this scale became a major industry, beyond the financial or organisational capacity of individuals who felt the call to enlighten public opinion. Wilks, Junius, Rochefort and others would have found it difficult in the days of the mass circulation dailies to air their views except as commentators on the pay roll of great newspaper magnates. Freedom of the press to which liberalism attached so much importance became a travesty in latter day liberalism.

Freedom of political beliefs and action is one of the essential ideas of liberalism. We may now see how much of it remained unaffected during the post Victorian period. No one, it is true, was denied the freedom of political opinion but the dominating fact in the political life that developed in England after 1870 was the strength of the party organisation. By the end of the century the party had to a very large extent become an instrument for enforcing conformity of views. The whip could not be disobeyed without grave consequences and if a member of the party desired to express opinion not in conformity with party views or to act according to his convictions which differed from what the majority held, he had to furrow a lonely plough with very little chance of making himself heard or felt in political life.

This again was the unforseen result of liberal action. The gradual enlargement of the franchise leading finally to adult suffrage created an electorate which consisted of the entire nation. Effective political action by the electorate became possible only through organised parties which, having to deal with millions of men, had naturally to be built up at enormous cost on a nationwide basis. Elections became costly affairs beyond the capacity of people of ordinary means. Political parties with large resources and with efficient ground organisation covering the entire country became an essential feature of democratic government. The control of the party over the individual became stricter as the individual became more and more dependent on the party for his election, and in fact for his effective participation in political life. This was no less true of America than of Britain. In France alone of the major liberal countries, the allegiance to the party continued to be weak, the reason being the multiplicity of parties and not a more live individualism in French political life. Local interests and influences were also greater in France All the same it would be true to say of French political life no less than of British and American that the individual counted for less and less and the party for more and more

Finally it may be said that in the period of its overwhelming success when superficially it appeared that liberalism had triumphed and society was being reorganised according to basic liberal ideas, the social, economic and political life in those countries which had seen their growth and fulfilment was being dominated increasingly by other principles True, liberal ideas were still there, but the state had become dominant and Herbert Spencer himself felt called upon in his later days to write a book entitled *Man vs the State* By the thoroughness of its fulfilment liberalism came under eclipse as a result of the logic of its own development.

IV

NEW HORIZONS

WITH the first shot that was fired in the Great War of 1914, the liberal age came to an end It was not that during the war the nations had forgotten the ideas to which they attached value It was perhaps too much to expect that when nations faced dangerous crises public conduct should conform to all the values to which people attached importance in peace time But the hysteria, persecution mania, the super-patriotism of charlatans who set the tone of popular opinion, men like Horatio Bottomley, showed that the temper of the age had changed in a way that nobody had foreseen The anger with which the British public, usually tolerant, greeted Bernard Shaw's *Common Sense About the War*, a criticism in the genuine liberal tradition, the persecution of Bertrand Russell, and the bitterness with which men like Ramsay Macdonald, E D Morel and others were pursued showed that a new age of intolerance, disregard for truth and exploitation of mass psychology had dawned on the world The extent to which this intolerance went may be judged from the fact that to hear "German" music was considered unpatriotic and the British royal family had to change its great and historic name of

Guelph to Windsor, as if race, descent and history could be changed by a change of name

The years that followed the war showed that the liberal era had truly ended and that a new period of history was being ushered in, the governing ideas of which and the social configuration resulting from them had not yet become clear The inter war period witnessed two significant developments Firstly, the stabilisation of the Russian Revolution together with the emergence of Communism not only as a social and political philosophy, but as a challenging ideal of political action, to which large sections of politically progressive opinion everywhere at the time looked up as their ideal—a new set of doctrines, values and principles of action covering the entire range of human activity, whose attraction, influence and authority were soon to become evident among large sections of people Secondly, a totalitarian, reactionary integration of society which denied the values of democracy and extolled dictatorship, swept over large portions of Europe, submerging all the Mediterranean countries (excepting France), Yugoslavia, Austria, Poland and Germany in an immense movement of opinion for which there is no parallel Fascism, as this movement came to be known, had a strange appeal to the middle classes in the countries where it gained authority There was one thing in common between Communism and

Fascism, which during this period seemed to face each other They both denied liberalism and democracy Those who had occasion to visit the Paris Exhibition of 1936 would remember how the Soviet and Nazi pavilions, both massive and striking in appearance, faced each other like snarling giants It was symbolic of the period In this epic struggle, liberalism did not seem to count at all Even in England and France, the traditional and historic homes of liberal thought, other doctrines now held sway Progressive opinion was represented by Socialism In France it was the period of the *croix de feu* and other crypto fascist movements which finally went down in disgrace during the Vichy interlude

It might appear strange that a political philosophy which had been considered almost axiomatic for nearly eighty years could have so suddenly been supplanted at the very first contact with the reality of war, yet that was the fact Liberalism, its enemies insisted, was a fair weather philosophy, a doctrine suited to conditions of peace and prosperity. It is true to some extent that it was a philosophy of optimism which grew up in a period when there was no widespread upheaval, an age when the European people overspread the world and the wealth of Asia flowed into the coffers of the Western nations Though during the first great period of liberalism there were the Crimean and the German Wars, apart from the American Civil War, they were limited conflicts which seemed hardly to affect the irresistible march towards national prosperity More-over the period between 1870 and 1914 was not marked by any war in Europe and though careful observers could have marked the growth of rivalry and the rising temper of the two blocs, Anglo French and Austro German, the public seemed to believe that human beings were rational enough to realise how foolish would be a war between the leading European nations and how disastrous its results would be to civilisation as a whole When the war broke out liberalism found itself unprepared to meet the crisis

During the period of the war liberalism was forgotten Nor was this surprising as the very first shot in the war exposed the illusion on which much of liberal philosophy was based, that progress in knowledge can be equated with progress in morality or to put it in another way, that with greater national wealth, greater production and greater comforts, mankind would become more reasonable and less prone to decide the future by the hazards of war During the four years and three months that war raged, the Western world learnt many lessons One of the most dangerous, nonetheless important, was how the stupidity of people could be organised against the reasonableness of the common man and how unscrupulous propaganda which during the war both sides had used with unexpected success could be made an instrument of government The manipulation of the subconscious had taken the place of appeal to reason Thus was Hitlerism born out of war time experience

An infinitely more important development had taken place during the war and that was the October Revolution The doctrine of Socialism had grown up during the liberal period It was indeed a parallel growth whose significance had been overlooked during most of the nineteenth century In the latter days of liberal dominance socialist ideas had, however, begun to influence liberal thought Before the war, Socialism had begun to operate as a leaven, a progressive minority view which had become influential with intellectuals, but with the great October Revolution the whole situation underwent a change From the first days of the Revolution it began to issue appeals to the proletariat of the world and to subject nations under colonial domination Also, once the Revolution in the Soviet Union was stabilised, Communism came to be looked upon by large sections of people everywhere as an alternative philosophy of life That the communists looked upon it as an inevitable development towards which all societies were moving by the compulsion of economic facts need not concern us here The significant thing is that Communism became a world wide movement challenging the very postulates of liberal society and offering an alternative in every field of life which appealed to considerable sections of people everywhere

Though this challenge was a growing one in the inter-war period, the disparity in power between the communist and the capitalist world obscured its importance Also, the Nazi Fascist totalitarian powers who, from the point of view of Western nations, were heresiarchs who threatened from inside the structure of western European society, began to claim anti Communism as the bond which united them The liberal democracies of the West were thus placed in a position of the gravest moral dilemma of the time The temporary alliance between the West and Communist Russia destroyed the more aggressive manifestations of Nazi power though the idea that totalitarian Fascism was eliminated from the world by this victory is obviously exaggerated in view of its continued and unashamed existence in Spain and Portugal From the Second World War, Communism not only emerged as a challenging world force claiming the allegiance of almost half the total population of the world, but putting forth even more dogmatically its ideals which totally repudiated the values of liberalism,

Was liberalism a forgotten creed during this period between 1919 and the present? It is undoubted that as an ideal it had ceased to appeal It had also ceased to have a working programme In the period after 1919, liberalism had no new message because its doctrines had been assimilated and become part of western European tradition Even in Germany and Italy, the Nazi period was no more than a hiatus arising from the despair of defeat in the case of Germany and of disillusionment in the case of Italy Western Europe broadly returned to the fold of liberal thinking though this was achieved at the cost of another and more disastrous world war In fact it may well be affirmed that it was the overwhelming success of liberal ideas that led to the eclipse of liberalism as a political creed Its fate as a political philosophy can be best described in the words of Aeschylus

"So, in the Libyan fables it is told
That once an Eagle stricken with a dart
Said, when he saw the fashion of the shaft
With our feathers and not by others hand
Are we now smitten"

There is another very important reason for the failure of liberal programmes after the first Great War The industrialisation of the Western countries led to the rise of the proletariat to great political power As we have noticed before, liberalism at different stages helped not only to organise the working classes, but extended political franchise to them and in the last stages even removed by legislation the legal obstacles which the courts had raised in the way of their march to political power With each step in the growth of the political power of the working classes liberalism became weaker and weaker The middle classes, who *par excellence* represented liberal thought, were unable to assimilate the proletariat however much they sympathised with the working classes in their demands for better life As Marx had emphasised, all thinking was socially conditioned and while leaders of the proletariat may come out of the middle classes, it is obvious that the thinking of the middle classes must necessarily reflect their class interests in whatever universal terms it may be clothed The incapacity of liberal middle classes to absorb the proletariat meant inevitably the eclipse of liberalism as a political programme though its basic doctrines might have become part of the thinking of non communist nations

That liberalism forms what may be called the matrix of the Western democracies, even when their political programmes are shaped to suit socialist creeds may be seen from the increasing differences between Communism and Democratic Socialism Both have broadly speaking a common origin Both accept the economic and social analysis of Marx And yet what is it that differentiates the socialist thinking of the West from the communist doctrines of the Soviet Union, China and other countries? It seems to me that the distinction between the Western and Soviet interpretations of Marx (what is known as Marxist Leninist doctrine) lies in the liberal background of Western thinkers To the Western socialist, liberal values are important though they no doubt require adjustment to changing conditions of economic life In the Marxist Leninist way of thinking these values are flatly denied on the ground that the freedoms so strongly advocated in liberal societies represent only the tactics of class struggle, that the supremacy of law on which liberalism exists and which Western socialists accept is nothing but the acceptance of crystallised versions of class morality It is unnecessary to examine these arguments at length The unbridgeable gulf between the communists and the rest of the world lies in their approach not so much to the discarded economics of liberalism, but to the liberal freedoms on which modern democratic societies have been built up

Has liberalism then no future beyond the limited one from being part of the great tradition of democratic life? The answer lies in the ability of liberal thinkers to find a reasonable adjustment with what is valid and of importance in Marxian thinking. The greatest liberal of our time, the philosopher John Dewey in a remarkable passage states, "I cannot find intellectual, moral or aesthetic satisfaction from the professed philosophy which animates Bolshevist Russia. But I am sure the future historian of our times will combine admiration of those who had the imagination first to see that the resources of technology might be directed by organised planning to serve chosen ends with astonishment at the moral and intellectual habitude of other peoples who were technically so much further advanced." (*Individualism Old and New*, p. 90.) This refusal to accept organised planning not only for achieving economic but social end which caused Dewey such astonishment may indeed be attributed to the hold that liberalism with its faith in individualism, initiative and private enterprise continues to have on society. But that opposition in most progressive countries became weak, as the economic and social achievements of planned societies became more and more marked. In England, France and Germany public ownership of sections of industry led in a measure to state planning while the social ends of economic planning like ensuring a more equal distribution of income, provision of essential social services at public cost, greater and ever increasing responsibility of the state for the welfare of all, especially the less privileged, became in fact essential parts of state s planned activity Liberalism had to adjust itself to planning much against its own past prejudices

If planning was against the idea of *laissez-faire* on which liberalism built up its prosperity, the great leviathan state with ever increasing functions, gradually covering all aspects of human activity, to the growth of which liberalism itself contributed not a little in its later stages, seems to be directly against some of the basic conceptions of liberalism As we have noticed, suspicion of the executive power of the state was one of the earliest ideas around which liberalism grew up It was no doubt as reaction against the autocratic power of the monarchies, as historically it was as a protest to the monarchical state and its powers that liberalism developed both in America and Europe Individualism was inscribed in letters of gold on the banners of liberalism but Mill himself had foreseen that the logical development in the case of a society of which industrialism had become the dominant characteristic was an administering state In the era following the first Great War the power of the state increased immensely Further, this became in a way a major characteristic of the period after the second

Great War I have described this tendency elsewhere in the following words

> "Every state in the world today is totalitarian, in the sense that it claims the totality of powers It was said in the beginning of the century that the modern state was Jenghiz Khan with the telegraph line Today it is much more than that It is Jenghiz Khan with distance control exercised by a hundred methods It speaks with a million voices on the radio It overhears our conversations on the telephone It pries into our secret thoughts by censoring our letters It controls the water we drink the food we eat, the light we use, our modes of transportation, and in fact practically everything in our lives It gives with one hand and takes away with the other In fact its picture is that of some demon of Hindu mythology multiplied manifold, a Ravana with a thousand faces and a million hands, each hand wielding a different instrument of power What chance has the individual against such an institution—impersonal, all pervasive, unmoved by sentiment, armed both by the power of the law and by every possible instrument of authority? The individual in the modern state, whether it be capitalist or communist, is reduced to a position of nullity"

This state of total power is not altogether a new conception The legists of the Hohenstaufen emperor Frederick II had enunciated a theory of sovereignty which combined the powers of the church and of the state in the emperor That dynasty however had to pay the heaviest penalty in history for enunciating so heretical a creed, for medieval Europe firmly believed as a self evident truth the existence of the twin cities of God and Man But after the Reformation the state begins to assume the combined authority and it finds theoretical justification in Bodin, Hobbes and other thinkers who formulated the theory of the omnipotent state Liberalism was to some extent a reaction against this view, but not from the point of view of the church or other intermediate bodies claiming loyalty like the nobility, the guilds or the boroughs, but of the individual The Liberal State was endowed with plenary legislative power As defined by Austin, it was all-embracing in its claims for legislative totality What liberal thinkers with the exception of John Stuart Mill rejected was the extension of the state's executive and administrative power

The fundamental contradiction in this attitude became clear in the last quarter of the 19th century when the original liberal formula for reform, public enquiry by commission, detailed report with evidence, legislation and inspectorate, was found to be too good a procedure not to be applied to the issues which came up before Parliament. Since then, the growth of administration has been so steady that today all the democratic states have raised on the matrix of liberalism an ever increasing complex of administrative machinery so as to justify the description that Professor Wheare gave to the British Government, that it is no more a parliamentary democracy but a parliamentary bureaucracy. How far we have travelled from the heyday of liberalism may be judged from the fact that Bagehot's classic description of the Constitution of England in the middle of the 19th century did not even allude to the administrative services considering them in fact unimportant from the point of view of constitutional power. At the beginning of the century Professor Dicey lecturing at Oxford on the Law of the Constitution also ignored the services. In fact he could never get over his surprise that the French, a liberal democratic nation, should have a system of administrative law which gave to the services a privileged position in relation to the ordinary citizen.

A similar transformation has taken place even in the United States which originally attempted to govern without a regular civil service. Today the situation is different. A proper federal service—unrelated to the political parties or the spoils system

—functions in Washington, and though the range of American administration is perhaps less pervasive, there is no doubt that the tendency is towards an expanding public service

Clement Attlee justifying this development declared in the House of Commons that the civil services have grown because the functions of government have grown that the public expect more things from the government now than in the past and the services the government renders have also grown immeasurably In fact the administrative state, enjoying total legislative powers and penetrating through its executive functions all aspects of human activity, is a characteristic of the age and liberalism if it has to function has to reconcile itself to it and adjust its doctrines to the new conditions

Also, it should be realised that the growth of this new leviathan state and the administrative despotism which is to some extent a characteristic of it, have other origins which make them broadly acceptable to the masses The suspicion and fear of financial and industrial power make the ordinary people look upon the state as their protector, as in former days the common people looked upon the monarchy for protection against feudal power The Tudor and Bourbon states claiming total power to themselves grew out of this fear against feudal power For the time, in the context of feudal anarchy, the growth of royal power was no doubt a progressive and liberal trend A similar situation arose as a result of the immense growth in industrial and financial power at the end of the 19th century The power of the new baronage of finance and industry was more comprehensive, more ruthless and less open to resistance than that of the feudal baronage No doubt the proletariat and the common people were able to develop some countervailing power, but with the identification of the people with the state, with the growth of democracy based on adult franchise, the people began to look upon the state as their champion and protector against the overweening power of industry and finance The danger of course was there that the state may identify itself with special interests—the doctrine to which an American industrialist, Mr Charles Wilson, gave magniloquent expression when he declared that what was good for the General Motors was good for the United States But the idea of the common man is different and broadly the common man is right, for sinister interests cannot for long control the policies of a popular government, especially where countervailing power is also well organised The existence and effective use of legislation like Sherman anti-trust laws and the increasing control of industry by the state are sufficient evidence to prove this The fact is that the growth of state power in conditions where the masses are identified with the state and exercise effective political power not only through their parliaments but at all levels of administration is a progressive and liberal development in the circumstances of today, for it is the one effective method of ensuring social justice The overwhelming power of economics on society is what Marx discovered and proclaimed Without its control and utilisation for social purposes the life of the common man will always be subject to arbitrary will of groups and classes With the enormous increase in economic activity and with the power which new machines place in the hands of those who control them, there is no alternative machinery today by which social justice can be ensured and freedom and development for the individual enforced outside the all-embracing state Liberalism, if it has to survive, has to adjust itself to this overriding fact of our times

The central problem of liberalism relates to the position of the individual The great war cries of the past, equality, liberty, fraternity, freedom of conscience, freedom of speech, etc were obviously rights which the individual in a liberal society was meant to enjoy Yet as we have seen these rights have at different times stood for different things

It is in the name of the individual's freedom that John Bright objected vigorously to the limitation of working hours for children It is again in the name of individual freedom that the claim of trade unions to act collectively was denied It was on the argument of the individual's right to property that the Supreme Court of the United States in a famous case upheld the right to own slaves If the liberal state has within a century given freedom to women prevented the exploitation of children and young persons regulated conditions of work in factories made it possible for labour to organise countervailing power to enforce compulsory education improve health conditions by compulsory vaccination inoculation etc in fact if it has been able to transform society in a manner in which the conditions for the common man are better than they were ever in the past it was in the face of the opposition of those who claimed to be the champions of individualism Indeed it could not be denied that each one of these major legislative measures involved encroachment on the rights of groups or individuals Even a measure like the Compulsory Education Act may be said to have encroached on the right of the parent to send his child to work and thus earn his keep

The weakness of the earlier conceptions of individualism lay in the fact that they were conceived as something to be preserved against the encroach ments of the state Even the doctrine of social contract seemed to postulate this view The problem of freedom and broadly of politics was thought of in terms of man *vs* the state Also the experience of previous ages when kings and nobles represented state or feudal power, the interference of superior authority appeared to be for personal or class interests With the change in the character of the state for which liberalism itself was to a large extent responsible, this attitude of individual's rights standing in opposition to the power of the state became devoid of meaning

The necessity for the social control of individuals has been recognised at all times Tribal traditions, law, *dharma*, church and similar controls were at all times necessary to safeguard the rights of the individual no less than to ensure the safety of society The earliest thinkers on social problems recognised that man can have his being and fulfilment only in society Otherwise according to the *Mahabharata* the *Matsya Nyaya*—the doctrine of the big fish eating the small one—will prevail One of the most eminent of modern liberal thinkers, Dr Radhakrishnan, in a notable speech at Shanghai emphasised that it was man in his solitude that was responsible for the greatest inventions, for the creation of objects of beauty, the composition of music, poetry, etc And yet no Robinson Crusoe in his deserted island has produced masterpieces or made revolutionary discoveries If Einstein in the solitude of his laboratory or study has a flash of inspiration which changes our ideas of the world, it is no disparagement of his individual genius to say that his flash of inspiration was possible only on the basis of the work of his innumerable predecessors If a poet is inspired in solitude to compose a poem of outstanding beauty, the language, the words and even the images which he uses are not the creations of his solitude but what he has inherited from society It is therefore meaningless to talk of pure individualism, of an individual standing apart from and against society, developing his full powers without the assistance of social forces and outside social controls

Though liberalism inherited an anarchical conception of individualism, its practice as we have noticed was at all times different From the earliest days of liberal power it set itself to free the individual through legislative and state action from the limitation that the rights of classes and groups established over the masses Today, if liberalism is to have any meaning, a new conception of individualism has to be formulated in relation to the state whose power is erected on the people as a whole Society now is organised on the basis of science and technology, and as against a society so organised the individual is helpless In the words of Dewey he is "a lost individual" if he places himself in opposition to a state so powerfully armed and so comprehensively organised as the modern state is The helplessness the individual feels against the state with its technical specialisation, bureaucratic organisation and scientific methods of controlling opinion is no doubt the reflection of a new and unfamiliar situation which he is called upon to face This feeling is due in a large measure to the traditional idea of looking upon the state as something organised outside ourselves and inimical to our liberty The liberalism of the future should provide the theory for a new integration of the individual with society and no doubt also with the intermediary groups which have become part of our society What is valuable and should be saved, if man is to remain free, is the individual s worth and not any particular freedom which can have meaning only in terms of the society in which we live In a passage which is worth quoting, Bertrand Russel has dealt with this problem ' There is need for a new doctrine on this subject of my duty to my neighbour It is not only traditional religious teaching that fails to give adequate guidance on this subject, but also the teachings of nineteenth century liberalism Take for example such a book as *Mill on Liberty* Mill maintains that which the state has a right to interfere with being those of my actions that have serious consequences to others it should leave me free where the effects of my actions concern only myself Such a principle, however, in the modern world leaves hardly any scope for individual freedom As society becomes more organic the effects of men on each other become more and more numerous and important so that there remains hardly any scope for individual freedom '

The fact is that in the changed circumstances individual freedom has to be defined not in relation to the state but in relation to intermediate groups and other individuals The state through law sets voluntary limits to its own power The rights of the individual against the state are no longer presumed to have an independent existence or to arise from any set of natural rights but from laws which the state itself has laid down which it can expand or restrict at will The individual therefore has to integrate himself with the new society and not consider himself as something in opposition to it When, however, it comes to his rights against other individuals or intermediary groups he looks to the state as the guardian of his rights It is this emphasis on the difference between the worth of the individual, his right to full development and expression within the state and the society and his freedom to be guarded against the encroachment by other individuals or groups and not the idea that the individual stands aside and apart from the state and the society that constitutes the new basis of liberalism

What, it may be asked is left of liberalism if it is to adjust itself to the leviathan state and if the old dogma of individualism as the continuing fight of man for his rights against the state is given up in favour of the new individual who has his being and finds his fulfilment within the state? The answer is that all this growth of the state, its manifold activities its pervasive interests and its all-embracing power is based in liberal societies on the matrix of social justice, supremacy of law on an enlarging conception of equality, and a live sense of protection and support to the masses against vested interests of individuals, groups and classes The new liberalism is in fact embodied in the welfare state which while giving fresh content to the old slogans of liberalism and inscribing them on its standard consciously tries to minimise economic inequalities to protect and develop individuality by the elimination of poverty, better conditions of life provision for education freer social relationships provision of security in old age etc What differentiates the welfare state from the Marxian state of the communists which also provides no less effectively for these things is the liberal basis of the welfare state

Perhaps it is necessary to emphasise at this stage that the liberalism of the future will be the outcome of the assimilation of socialist conceptions of economic equality brought about by conscious use of state power through planning and otherwise, and a classless society brought about by the control of economic forces by the state

The great distinction between the liberalism of the nineteenth and the earlier decades of the twentieth century and the liberalism of today relates essentially to the attitude to the middle classes As we have noticed earlier, liberalism of the mid-nineteenth century identified the state with the middle classes Though it helped to develop the working classes and enabled the proletariat to grow and feel self conscious it failed to absorb them The new liberal thought does not identify itself with the middle classes for it has, however reluctantly, come to realise that the elimination of economic inequality is the ideal towards which society is inevitably moving The middle classes constitute therefore a diminishing force in all progressive societies, gradually passing on to the proletariat the culture which they had developed during the last three hundred years and which no less than their financial resources had separated them from the working classes.

In western European countries where the liberal revolution had already taken place, this transition from the middle class liberalism of the past to the new liberalism of the welfare state was almost unseen and unchallenged. It is in the newly independent countries of Asia that the new liberalism finds itself challenged by the values of Communism. Communism becomes an alternative to the liberal welfare state in countries where there is no strong liberal and therefore no democratic tradition. It is a most significant fact which requires to be emphasised that the spectacular success of Communism during the last forty years has been confined to countries which have had no liberal tradition behind them. The only apparent exception is Czechoslovakia where the liberal experiment had been tried only for less than sixteen years. In the vast territories of the Soviet Union, in the new democracies on their European borders, in China and other areas in Asia where Communism has taken root and may be said to be flourishing, there was never any liberal tradition either native to the soil as in western Europe or which came to existence through foreign impacts as in India, Ceylon, Burma and Egypt. The marginal areas in Asia and Africa where the conflict between democracy and Communism is going on are those where the liberal revolution was never attempted and the values of liberalism had no hold on the people

The case of India is particularly interesting The liberal tradition in India has the longest history outside western Europe and the USA Ram Mohan Roy the founder of that tradition was so to say an adopted child of the Enlightenment of the eighteenth century He was even said to have been in correspondence with Condorcet Very few people even in India know that Ram Mohan gave a great banquet in Calcutta to celebrate the liberal revolution in Spain, a false dawn which created a short-lived optimism in many liberal minds From this early period the Indian revival was marked by two essentially liberal characteristics an urge for social reform, and a secular attitude towards politics

It also deserves to be mentioned that there was another stream which helped to swell the liberal current in India The growth of the liberal spirit in England began to be reflected, no doubt in a weak and diluted manner, in the official policies of England in India Macaulay, that staunch and unbending apostle of liberalism, was responsible for two of its most important manifestations a Penal Code which established the equality of all, the Brahmin and the Pariah and the Raja and the peasant before the law, and an educational system which opened up to Indian youth the great traditions of liberal thought which were then beginning to find expression in English literature These two parallel traditions combined to create the intellectual basis of the national movement in India, which to the very end upheld the liberal principles of its origin and embodied them in noble and enduring words in its Constitution

Broadly this analysis is true of new Japan, Ceylon, Burma, Pakistan, the Philippines, Thailand and Egypt Contact with liberal Europe in the nineteenth and early twentieth centuries and the establishment, no doubt modified to a degree by colonial conditions, of liberal institutions have led to the growth of societies which have the roots of liberalism in them even where the forms are not democratic

A major consequence of the hold of liberalism in these countries has been the failure of Communism to gain influence over the masses Even where the communists are allowed to function freely as in India, Ceylon and Burma their influence has been limited and they present no major threat to the political life of these countries In fact some observers have noticed indications of a modification of their approach to many problems in view of the value which the common people attach to liberal freedoms which Communism had long been inclined to reject as experiences of bourgeois morality or interest Whether such a modification is being worked out or not, it is impossible to say but it is obvious as we know from the experience of western European countries that Communism which fails to take notice of liberal values, no doubt modified by the circumstances of a classless society, has but little chance against democracy

Earlier I had quoting from Dewey, expressed the astonishment of the future historians "at the moral and intellectual habitude of those who had not the imagination to see the value" of organised planning I am sure the same historians would not fail to be astonished at the blindness of the great minds who could plan and organise such tremendous feats as the navigation of outer space and the projection into unknown beyond of sputniks and luniks and reshape a backward society in such a way as to catch up and leave behind the most advanced countries in technology, I repeat historians could not fail to be astonished at the blindness of the great men in regard to the necessity of freedom of thought and conscience for the true development of man , that they should fail to analyse correctly, why the same doctrines which animate millions of people with more than religious zeal in countries which had no liberal traditions should have so little appeal to others with a liberal background

May be, that a faint light has already begun to penetrate the communist world in the same way as many ideas of Communism are penetrating into liberal thought The doctrine of co existence itself, however you may interpret it, involves the acceptance of a compromise The abortive Hundred Flowers movement was no less significant

Both the communist ideology and its opposite point of view which is not capitalism but liberalism are, it seems to me, moving slowly from their entrenched positions The new liberalism, which is steadily incorporating the social ideals, the economic planning, the creation of a classless society by the gradual elimination of economic inequalities and the control by the state of the industries on which the power dynamism in society depends has already transformed itself without losing its traditional values In short the welfare state is the present day version of liberalism The most conservative states of today are slowly moving towards it and what is more, it is the only alternative that is open to the newly liberated states if they desire to maintain their identity and at the same time advance towards the goal of social and economic progress.

V

LIBERALISM AND THE FUTURE

IN THE preceding lectures we have endeavoured to trace the growth of liberal thought, the hold it had over the minds of people for over a century, the political and social programmes that it initiated and finally its eclipse in the period that followed the first Great War We have also emphasised how some of its doctrines and ideas have passed into the common thought of the democratic half of the world and remain the basis of everyday life But its period of political authority is over There is no specifically liberal programme which awaits social or political realisation Though liberalism as a creed has merged into the tradition of life and has no need to be defended in democratic societies except when under attack by special interests, the importance of cultivating the liberal attitude in social and political life continues to be as important as ever

What is the liberal attitude? It is an open approach to problems, a curiosity towards and interest in new ideas, and a continuous endeavour to evaluate them in terms of the individual's position in society What the liberal attitude *is not* can be defined even more easily than what it is

It is not a dogmatic, closed mind It is not a defence of the *status quo*, nor an idealisation of the past The liberal attitude is best defined in a *sloka* by the great Sanskrit poet, Kalidasa, who says "Nothing is to be considered as good merely on the ground of its being old, nor is something to be rejected on the ground of being new The wise man accepts as good that which he finds so after trial" It is this open approach to the new in the realm of ideas that constitutes the liberal attitude and which progressive societies at all times have to cherish Bertrand Russell has pointed out with his usual penetration that the antithesis of liberalism is not conservatism but fanaticism "The liberal creed in practice," he says, "is one of live and let live, of toleration and freedom as far as public order permits, of moderation and absence of fanaticism in political matters Even democracy when it becomes fanatical ceases to be liberal" (*Philosophy and Politics*, p 71)

It is obvious that authority based on dogma, political, religious or economic, cannot be a part of the liberal attitude It may be a right approach in regard to religion when revelation or dogma is final or authoritative That does not concern our discussion So far as social, economic and political problems are concerned argumentation based on quotation from texts can mean nothing to a liberal and goes against the liberal attitude Whether such quotation comes from Marx, Lenin or Mao, or from what great liberal statesmen of the past had laid down as their creed, is of little importance There is no revealed book for the liberal This is important as the world today is facing a new set of conditions which no political thinker had foreseen and for which neither religious nor social provision had ever been made Undoubtedly we are passing into a new era where the old values have not the same meaning and the new problems are not only very vast in size and complicated in character, but are not governed by any precedent of which we have experience Also it is important to remember that the change from liberalism to the new world was not by a slow transition It was sudden and cataclysmic and covered not merely our political, social and economic lives, but our knowledge of physical sciences, our conceptions of space and time In fact it touched the most fundamental aspects of our thought and life It is an uncharted sea that we have entered and we are not equipped with sufficiently tested instruments to enable us to navigate freely and safely

It is a characteristic of this sudden change from one period to another, from a period of settled morality, relationships and a general view of the world to a new one where nothing seems certain and vast possibilities open up, that people should feel pessimistic and claim that the world is out of joint Especially does such pessimism seem natural if an era of startling and revolutionary changes follows a period of widespread prosperity and optimism, as in the case of the century before 1914 To those who live through this period of confusion and of kaleidoscopic changes, it naturally appears as something tragic, confused and without a guiding philosophy Voices of reaction, generally represented by theologians and the moralists of history, talk in terms of the necessity of a return to Belief Maritain, Collingwood, Niebhour and others who see the hand of God in history appeal to a strengthening of faith, presumably their own, as the true solution to the challenging problems of the period The fact is that the world is witnessing the birth of a new era in which every aspect of political, social and economic life is undergoing change and rival philosophies of life are being worked out with conviction and enthusiasm Whatever old fashioned men may feel, it cannot be said that the age of sputniks, luniks and space travel, of atomic energy and nuclear science is an age which should make us pessimistic about the human race A new civilisation is undoubtedly taking shape It is foolish to believe that this new civilisation will be based on a single set of ideas or a complex of doctrines associated with any single school of thought, economic, philosophical or religious The inheritance of humanity is varied, complex and rich, tracing its origin to different sources No new doctrine can wholly displace the values of the old, nor can the old completely shut its doors to the new The Soviet Union and the communist states elsewhere cannot fail to be influenced and shaped by the values of the past ages of culture any more than the U S A and the other liberal democracies fail to absorb many of the values of the great civilisation developing under communist leadership We who live in this period of rival ideologies seem to be oblivious of the forces which help to minimise the present differences that are taking place no doubt slowly—almost imperceptibly—to create a middle ground between the two

The Swiss philosopher Ropke in his book, *The Social Crisis of our Time*, points out that not even the wisest of his generation is able to characterise accurately a period of change in which he is living "Can any one seriously imagine," he asks, "Lorenzo Medici one day stopping Boticelli in the streets of Florence and confiding to him his discovery that they are now living in the Renaissance?" In fact as an acute observer Lorenzo would no doubt have noticed much evidence of a break down in social values which would perhaps have disconcerted him

Though we are unable to see and evaluate as a whole the immense and unprecedented changes taking place in our own time, we cannot fail to observe certain obvious characteristics which differentiate the present age from the past I shall allude here only to such of them as are relevant to our discussion of the liberal attitude In the first place it is obvious that the seats of power in science, industry and social dynamics have shifted from their traditional centres London, Paris and Berlin, to other areas both East and West This does not mean that western Europe has lost its importance, but no longer are the nations of Europe the unquestioned leaders of the new world This is not without basic significance Paris London and other capitals of western Europe which had in the period of liberalism provided the light did so on the basis of a humane tradition which had a fairly long history It had also a unity of thought which gave to the experience of western Europe in the nineteenth century a sense of universality, no doubt exaggerated but significant enough to be of value The new civilisation which is growing up away from the great centres of European life is not subject in the same way to the traditions of the past

A second and related fact is that during the last quarter of a century the political world has expanded manifold In the nineteenth century only

Europe and the U S A counted in political world The inter war period witnessed the awakening of Asia but its liberation came only after the second Great War It has now been followed by the emergence of the African states The political community today consists of states in different stages of evolution spread over the five continents Their reaction to political ideas differs widely, but the fact cannot be overlooked that in the world of today the appeal that new ideas have to this growing body of non European people will determine their development Whether the liberal attitude, as we have defined it, *will continue seriously to influence* mankind in the future will depend on the appeal it has for the new nations

There is another major fact which deserves to be emphasised in this connection Liberalism is a philosophy of prosperity The liberal age so far as western Europe and U S A were concerned was an age of industrial development and production—the age of unprecedented prosperity It was the creed of an expanding middle class which did not suffer from hunger The emergent world of Asia and Africa consists of hungry millions for whom the philosophy of liberalism may not have the same appeal The real point which we cannot forget is that liberalism for all its appeal to humane sentiments had no solution for the problem of poverty As we have noticed, the eclipse of liberalism in western Europe was due to its failure to absorb the proletariat which it had by its policies aroused from its slumbers A similar problem faces it in the new world of Asia and Africa The new states have first to solve their problem of hunger A few countries like India may be able to escape the dilemma by a process of rapid industrialisation but the requirements of modern industry—adequate natural resources, developed technological skill and capacity to absorb and utilise the discoveries of science—these are not available in many of the states which are at the same time ground down by their poverty and held back by their own backwardness The appeal of Communism ordered, disciplined, utilising under an iron direction the total forces of the community for its economic betterment, would seem almost to be irresistible in these circumstances

There is also the problem of the peasantry The liberal attitude is, it has to be emphasised once again, an urban attitude, an attitude of a commercial and industrialised society The new states of Asia and Africa would continue to be dominantly peasant societies except perhaps in China and India where rapid industrialisation may affect agricultural production also Nowhere has the liberal attitude been characteristic of a peasant society though no doubt with the methods of mass communication available now and the power of the urban communities in the government of the state the inherent conservatism of the peasantry may in time become a tradition of the past.

It is not only the problem of hunger and the conservatism of the peasantry that stand in the way of the liberal attitude. It is also the problem of fear. We have noticed that the growth of liberalism was during a period of comparative peace when the great western European nations felt no sense of insecurity. But in the inter-war period when Nazism was menacing the world, and Communism also posed its great challenge, the world began to feel a new sense of insecurity. The period following the Second War witnessed the growth of a sense of fear as a major psychological factor among the nations. It is significant that Mr. Roosevelt's Atlantic Charter should include freedom from fear as one of the four basic freedoms which man had a right to look forward to. It is not only the Soviet Union and its allies that felt that their new life was being threatened by the capitalist powers of the world. The other powers, the liberal democracies, the great nations which had built up through centuries an open society and a free life began to be frightened of some thing they knew not. A sense of fear began to dominate them.

Fear is the enemy of the liberal attitude There is no use preaching tolerance moderation fair play and other virtues of the liberal mind to a man in the grip of fear Similar is the case with nations During the First War England witnessed absolutely preposterous exhibitions of national intolerance based on fear They would seem unbelievable today But one case deserves to be recalled because of its extreme absurdity A certain Pemberton Billing suddenly attained national prominence by making wild accusations of national treachery against persons in the highest society and by claiming to possess information about a Black Book in which the names of those personages who were alleged to be in the pay of the Germans were entered The strange thing was not that Pemberton Billing should have made these allegations but that they should have been widely believed and that Billing himself should have been acquitted by the Jury when prosecuted for libel The phenomenon of Macarthyism in post war America where for a time life was not easy for a man accused of holding liberal opinions proves the same fact that fear and liberalism find it impossible to live happily together

The present age undoubtedly is an age of fear A vague and menacing sense of uncertainty seems to hang over humanity The great nations of the West are afraid not merely of the overpowering might of the Soviet Union but of subversion from inside They are also vaguely apprehensive of the power of the new ideas which, they feel, creep upon them and weaken their resistance The communist states on their side fear the serried might of the capitalist nations whose policies are frankly based on the balance of nuclear terror So far as the liberated nations are concerned they have the growing fear that with the ever-widening gulf of technological skills and scientific knowledge their political freedom will in time become no more than nominal The present, in spite of its unprecedented achievements in science, its man in outer space, its shot at the moon, etc is the age of the Great Fear

What chance has the liberal outlook in these circumstances? Chief Justice Earl Warren in dealing with the refusal of a Club to put on its notice board the Bill of Rights on the ground that it was a controversial document expressed the doubt whether these famous amendments to the Constitution would have been passed by the legislature in our own day The very fact that appeals to the Fifth Amendment which lays down that a man cannot be forced to incriminate himself are frowned upon by large sections of otherwise enlightened people would show the extent to which fear has influenced public minds It is some times thought that a strong judiciary would provide the safeguards for liberal freedoms and would help to main tain the liberal attitude to public matters even when menaced by the dark forces of fear, suspicion and mistrust

But is this hope justified? True, the judiciary as a body consists of men trained to fairness of judgement, to keep their minds above the prejudices and passions of the common people and to uphold even against popular feeling both natural rights where such are assumed to exist and the rights enshrined in fundamental laws But after all judges are not beings from another world The general moods and tenses of a people, their fears and appre hensions affect them also, though perhaps to a lesser degree

This brings us to a new and dangerous characteristic of our time which in periods of crisis may over whelm all liberal attitudes and assist to set at large the darker forces in the human mind Advert isement is today a perfected technique which draws upon psychology, art, the exploitation of the sub conscious and other methods of influencing human action Also it has at its disposal the means of mass communication, cinema, radio, television, etc Many highly educated leaders of thought in our time consider advertisement as one of the basic features of modern economies, in so far as it is through the instrumentality of advertisement that new wants are created and met However that be, the importance of advertisement in modern life is something which cannot be overlooked Now what is the technique of advertisement? It is nothing short of the exploitation of the baser characteristics of the human mind, envy, desire to shine before others, etc So far as this new method of approach to the people is confined to the sale of goods, or to the creation of wants, it may, at least in one aspect of it, be looked upon as an aid to greater production on which the prosperity of nations is supposed to depend

But today advertisement is not confined to the economic sphere Public relations have become an essential aspect of politics So the methods suited to the promotion of sales are brought into play in controlling public mind The growing centres of private power in society utilise this method consciously in their interest, and the state itself by establishing a monopoly of radio and television and control over cinemas enters in a large way in the creation of public opinion Against these powerful interests exploiting the baser qualities of man, his cupidity, his fear, his envy of others, the liberal attitude would seem to be fighting a losing battle

There are, however, many elements in the situation

which lead us to hope that the situation may not be as black as it looks In the first place in the democratic half of the world there is still a living faith in liberal values, though their realisation is becoming more and more difficult as the machinery suited to the new age through which these values could operate, have yet to be evolved The real danger however comes from the gradual disappearance of the the middle classes with their belief in the liberal values In the welfare state of the future, working consciously towards the abolition of social inequalities, the weakening, if not the total obliteration, of the middle classes seems to be inevitable How then could these values which are associated basically with the middle classes survive even if they have in a general way become a part of the common tradition?

It is obvious that without a conscious effort on the part of the new leadership these values will not survive As there is a general desire in democratic societies that the liberal attitude should survive and the great freedoms which liberalism has given to the world should endure, even when its social and economic institutions are replaced by something more suited to the urges of the time, the problem that faces society is one of evolving suitable methods not merely to ensure the survival, but to strengthen the foundations of the liberal attitude How can this be done? Primarily through the promotion of a class devoted to the cultivation of human values, standing independent of current economic values but with social prestige high enough for them to uphold their ideas The continued emphasis on a humanistic education, the independence of universities and other centres of higher learning and thought, assured dignity and honour to professions like teaching, law and judiciary and to groups like poets, authors and artists whose vocations are financially not highly remunerative but are socially of the highest value—these will ensure in a democratic society adequate strength to the liberal attitude and continued supply of liberal thought suited to new conditions One of the most encouraging things during the painful period of Macarthyism in the United States was the firmness with which most of the great universities rallied to the defence of the professors In the same way in France during the height of reactionary pressure against the sympathisers with the Algerian nationalists, the universities stood firm in their defence of academic freedom In fact the universities where humanistic studies are encouraged have at all times been the breeding grounds of liberal thought I should not be understood as pleading for a humanistic education as against scientific studies In the modern world no country which does not make adequate provision for scientific studies at all levels has the least chance of achieving progress But it does not mean that humanistic studies should be neglected There is and should be a place of honour in every university for such studies, not merely because of the value of the disciplines involved, but because they emphasise the worth of the individual and are built round his rights in society The fact is that without encouragement to the study of humanities there can be no liberal attitude